The Golden Age of Amelia Island

Suzanne Davis Hardee

The Golden Age of Amelia Island

Suzanne Davis Hardee

Revised, Updated and Edited by
Kathleen Hardee Arsenault

Library of Congress Control Number: 2009938650

Hardee, Suzanne Davis 1922-2004
Arsenault, Kathleen Hardee 1947-

ISBN: 978-1-93-440105-7

Published by Lexington Ventures
107 Centre Street
Fernandina Beach, FL 32034

Printed in the United States of America
Walsworth Publishing Company
306 N. Kansas Ave.
Marceline, MO 64658

Layout, Typesetting and Publication Assistance:
Jan H. Johannes.

Cover Design:
Thomas R. Johannes of TRJ Digital Media.

Table of Contents

The Newport of the South:

Wars and Alarums:

The Last Glimmers of the Golden Age:

Index

Additional books by the staff and friends of the Amelia Island Museum of History in this series:

Found in Fernandina: The Magic of Museum Making, by Deon L. Jaccard.

Clash of the Cultures: The Awakening of History for Amelia Island, Florida, by Deon L. Jaccard.

David Levy Yulee: A Man and His Vision, by Celeste H. Kavagaugh.

The Golden Age of Amelia Island: The Churches, by Suzanne Davis Hardee.

Author's Introduction

Some years ago, for the benefit of the Amelia Island Museum of History, I was one of a small group of friends who promised to research and write about a specific part of the monumental history of Amelia Island. The members of the group were challenged to write about the rich African-American heritage of the island; David Levy Yulee; the Golden Age; and other aspects of the colorful history represented by the eight flags that have fluttered through centuries of Amelia Island's storms and gentle breezes. I was assigned the era of the island's Golden Age, a time that I believe may be roughly measured from the year 1869, when the last Federal troops departed from Fort Clinch, to the first decades of the twentieth century, when the island's remarkable postwar prosperity began to fade.

In writing of the Golden Age, I found the subject to be so broadly revealing that I separated my material into two small booklets previously published by the Museum. In my first booklet, I tried to impart a glimpse of what the beautiful island of Amelia was like in its so-called Golden Age. I hoped to whet the appetite of the reader to learn more about the Golden Age men and women, their homes, churches, schools, and places of business. The first booklet is thus entitled *The Golden Age of Amelia Island—A Glimpse*. In the second booklet, *Churches of the Golden Age of Amelia Island,* I wrote of the churches of the period—a subject that stands on its own, rich with history, and, I believe, rich with still untapped resources.

In this third book, I attempt to show the reader how the Golden Age of Amelia Island sprouted, budded, and blossomed from Reconstruction years through a time of reconciliation and prosperity. I have tried to broaden my writing on the Golden Age into more than a glimpse. In doing this, I endeavored to reap a selective harvest of Golden Age information from a variety of documents and publications and from dear friends and relatives who have made their documents, pictures, and newspaper clippings available to me. Most especially though, I have gleaned full measure, pressed down, and overflowing from the pages of the *Florida Mirror*, the leading Fernandina newspaper published from 1878 to 1900. As I poured over the microfilmed, laminated, and fragile original pages of the *Florida Mirror*, so many people, institutions, landmarks, and events of the Golden Age shone forth to inspire me. The *Mirror* is the true delight of local historians.

The Golden Age is only a part of the history of Amelia Island. It is hoped that in the near future the other eras of the island's remarkable history will one day be written by local historians and published by the Museum; in particular, that of African American history on Amelia Island.

Suzanne D. Hardee

Editor's Note

As the eldest of Suzanne Davis Hardee's five daughters, it was my privilege to inherit the task of finishing her third book on the history of Fernandina, the book that she envisioned as a successor to her two previous books on the city's "Golden Age." *The Golden Age of Amelia Island: A Glimpse* was published in 1993, followed by *Churches of the Golden Age of Amelia Island* in 1994. In the ten years before her death in 2004, she traveled to libraries and archives in Tallahassee, Gainesville, and St. Augustine and spent endless hours pouring over crumbling Fernandina newspapers, particularly George Fairbanks's *Florida Mirror,* to complete her research on a culminating work on the Golden Age. Like Fernandina's famous visitor President Ulysses S. Grant, she continued to labor over the book that she intended as a legacy to her family and friends until the last days of her final illness.

The drafts of chapters my mother passed on to me ranged from the preliminary to the polished and from the early nineteenth century until the late 1930s. It became clear to me that the heart of her work was her chapters on the history of Fernandina from the end of Union occupation in 1869 to the last flares of the city's Golden Age that produced the 1915 Keystone Hotel, now demolished, and the graceful 1912 Post Office, the pride of downtown Fernandina. I have therefore limited this work to these "Golden Years" and rearranged the order of her original chapters. In this new format, historical chapters entitled "Reconciliation" and

"Reconstruction" are followed by topical sections focusing on "Making a Living," "Building a Modern City," "The Newport of the South," "Wars and Alarums," and "The Last Glimmers of the Golden Age."

My mother intended the following chapters to honor the people, institutions, and landmark events of Fernandina's Golden Age that live through the pages of the *Florida Mirror* and the documentary sources in her beloved archives of the Amelia Museum of History. Significant aspects of Fernandina's political, economic, and social history, particularly the story of the city's black citizens that was so dimly glimpsed in public records and newspapers, await fuller exploration.

This book is dedicated, as I believe my mother would have wished, to her beloved sisters and daughters, and to my beloved sisters, daughters, and aunts.

Kathleen Davis Hardee Arsenault
November 25, 2005

Reconciliation

Beneath the ashes of the Civil War, Fernandina lay
devastated, its docks, shops, and warehouses destroyed
and mountains of charred lumber towering over its
waterfront. Perversely, the devastation was caused not by
the conquering army's guns of war, but by the deliberate
action of fleeing Confederates who wished to leave behind
no materials or provisions intact for use by Union forces.

At the suggestion of General Robert E. Lee, the
Confederate government had given orders that Fernandina
and other Florida coastal cities should be evacuated and left
to the mercy of the U. S. Navy. Florida's few Rebel forces
could then move inland to protect the state's interior from
invasion. Civilians were urged to leave their homes and seek
protection in these Confederate-controlled areas. On March
3, 1862, David L. Yulee, Florida visionary, former United
States Senator, and builder of the Florida Railroad between
Fernandina and Cedar Key, dodged Yankee bullets on the last
train out of Fernandina. The next day, Confederates burned
the drawbridge connecting Amelia Island to the mainland
side of the river and began the sad task of dismantling inland
railroad tracks to keep Federal troops from using Yulee's
railroad to gain access into the interior of the state.

Alice Youngblood, in research notes for *Seeing Fernandina*,
ascribes the destruction of facilities along the waterfront to
"enraged secessionists" determined to ensure that "lumber
mills, etc., mostly owned by Northerners, were given to the
flames." In the words of Commodore Samuel P. Dupont,

in his report on the capture of Amelia Island, March 3, 1861, Confederate loyalists carried out this destruction so vindictively that the Union reconnaissance was literally guided by "pillars of fire by night and clouds of smoke by day."

After Lee's surrender, the Fernandina citizens who had fled the Union forces in 1862 returned home to find their properties confiscated for unpaid taxes; their Lieutenant Governor Abraham K. Allison and former Senators David L. Yulee and Stephen R. Mallory imprisoned; and their state under martial law. Confederate Governor John Milton had committed suicide in despair on April 1, 1865. Fernandina's governmental institutions were in the hands of Unionists, some, no doubt, wearing the mantle of overzealous and judgmental victors. Even the churches of the town were in the hands of the conquerors. Newly freed black Fernandinians strove to adapt to a drastically rearranged social order.

Of particular gall to the returning Confederates was the Freedmen's Bureau, established to administer civil and social justice to the freed slaves. Officials of the Bureau negotiated contracts between the freedman and his employer and dispensed food, medicine, agricultural supplies, and succor to newly free people who struggled to find their way in a world transformed. Reconciliation between races, and between victor and conqueror, would be a long soul-wrenching journey.

The altruistic aim of the Freedmen's Bureau was often corrupted, at least to Southerners' eyes, by the power and greed of its administrators. Among its duties, the Bureau was placed in charge of properties confiscated from Confederate sympathizers in occupied territory by the Direct Tax Commission enacted June 7, 1862. Under the Commission, Confederate property could be sold at auction to the highest bidder after being advertised for unpaid taxes.

Notices were therefore placed in Fernandina's Unionist newspaper, the *Peninsular,* but the announcements were of little use to Fernandina property owners who had fled behind Union lines. Unprincipled Bureau officials used the seized properties as an opportunity to obtain houses and acreage at bargain prices for their own benefit. The Commission sold tax-delinquent Amelia Island properties at auction as early as June 1863, and as late as sixteen years later, the courts were still clogged with the task of settling "war tax-sale claims" (*Florida Mirror,* Oct. 25, 1879).

A typical example is revealed in documents dated August 30, 1869, still held by the family of the Reverend Archibald Baker, first minister of the Presbyterian Church. After the Baker family left Fernandina before Federal occupation, their abandoned home at 112 North Sixth Street was used to quarter Union soldiers. The papers show Baker's early attempts to regain his property after it had been sold at a direct tax auction to A. E. Kinne, of Syracuse, New York. Although *The Florida Mirror* of January 19, 1884, stated that "complications growing out of the war and war legislation have now passed away, and by action of the government and courts the title to property in Fernandina may be considered to be permanently settled and well assured," it was not until January 11, 1895, that the Reverend Baker's claim was finally resolved when the Florida state government made a financial reimbursement to his estate.

Copies of documents housed in the Amelia Island Museum of History dated December 21, 1866, list properties owned by island Confederates that had been auctioned by the Direct Tax Commission. Certain names on the lists of Confederate property owners remain prominent on Amelia Island today, as do certain names listed as the purchasers of these bargain-rate properties. One eyebrow-raising example of a direct tax sale was that of former Confederate commander of Florida General Joseph Finegan's large, three-story mansion, purchased for just $25 by Freedman's Bureau teacher Chloe Merrick. Although benefiting from a fire sale bargain price and assisted by Florida's Direct Tax Commissioner Harrison Reed, Chloe Merrick's intent was noble: she established and administered an orphanage for children of former slaves in the Confederate general's mansion, in addition to founding schools in Fernandina for the children of freed blacks. Merrick was the sister-in-law of A. E. Kinne who purchased the Archibald Baker house noted above.

Florida Memory Project
Florida Department of State

Freedman's Bureau teacher Chleo Merrick.

The Freedmen's Bureau and the Direct Tax Commission, often poorly and unwisely administered, became riddled with graft. When overzealous officials of the Bureau were believed to have made blatant attempts to control the Negro vote, their efforts generated deep hostility among the former Confederates who found themselves virtually disenfranchised by the Fourteenth Amendment of the Constitution, possibly the bitterest pill of their defeat. This amendment, proposed on June 16, 1866, prohibited the avowed Confederate from holding office in local and state governmental affairs, and forced on him the added humiliation of seeing his former slaves exercising their new rights to vote and hold office. At the polls, the former slave became the master. Black Republican political control, however, was short-lived. In the 1876 election of Democratic governor

George Drew, Florida's white Democrats returned to power, a dominance that endured until the Civil Rights movement of the 1960s.

In Fernandina and Nassau County, few complete records remain of African Americans holding administrative positions immediately after the war. Fortunately, however, some of the men who served as aldermen, marshals, assessors, and tax collectors during the Reconstruction years are still locally remembered. Among them are Samuel Petty, John Stays, Roman Cribb, Ray Delaney, Edward Mordecai, Robert MacDonell, Peter Williams, and Riley Robinson. These men ultimately earned the respect and esteem of white Fernandinians—the respect and esteem begrudgingly bestowed. Their significant contributions to the Reconstruction era, however, have been increasingly recognized by modern Florida historians. But to those who had fought for the "southern way of life," it was no small trial to see city, county, and state government in the hands, no matter how capable, of former slaves, not to mention the hated white carpetbaggers. Reconciliation was, to all, a slow and painful journey.

Florida Memory Project
Florida Department of State
NO 29093

Brigadier General Joseph Finegan

5

In varying degrees, an uneasy postwar atmosphere prevailed everywhere in the South. On Amelia Island, the postwar uneasiness was not due entirely to what former Confederates considered unsavory carpetbagger and Freedmen's Bureau practices in the local governmental institutions. Confederate sympathizers earned their just share of blame for the postwar unrest.

A glimpse of the Reconstruction era's trials and tribulations may be seen in a collection of letters written from Fernandina by Daniel Richards to his Illinois Congressman, Elihu B. Washbourne. Richards was a long-suffering self-proclaimed "carpetbagger" stationed on Amelia Island after the war. In his "Letters of a Carpetbagger in Florida, 1866-1869," published in the *Florida Historical Quarterly* in January 1958, Richards complained that his mail was being rifled by rebel "mean devils....old blockade runners, and pirates who three times rammed the mail boat delivering mail to the island." He writes of "Joseph Finegan, an unpardoned Major General who is doing more to keep up and create bad feelings between parties here, and especially toward all Union men, than any other man in Florida. I consider him the leading rebel in Florida." Richards wrote on May 12, 1866, that "it is not safe to withdraw the military from the State for a long time to come."

The Civil Rights Bill [enacted by Congress in March 1866] can only be enforced at the point of a bayonet. Only yesterday afternoon, a colored woman called at a rebel drugstore for a dose of medicine...[but] before she got home... she sunk down and died before dark....The agent of the Freedmen's Bureau is having a postmortem examination today." Richards's letter to his congressman reveals the tense situation caused by the woman's death. "The leading rebels made a great parade of buying buckshot yesterday very publicly." Clearly Daniel Richards did not trust rebels to obey the Civil Rights Bill, nor did he trust rebels with the mails, as druggists, or with buckshot.

In 1869, however, Union soldiers left Fort Clinch, leaving only Ordnance Sergeant John Barr in charge. With the removal of Federal troops, the rebuilding of Amelia Island began in earnest. Although carpetbagger Daniel Richards called it "madness and folly"—former Confederates likely used the same epithet—the state constitution adopted that year became the foundation, however shaky, for the government found in Tallahassee today. The ratification of the constitution offered "all men" the right to vote. The new constitution established schools for the deaf and blind, a hospital for the insane, a state prison, and a homestead tax exemption. Fernandina and the state of Florida were recovering slowly but surely from the "late unpleasantness."

Amelia Island's amazing recovery after the war unquestionably can be credited to David Yulee. Island prosperity began to take hold following Yulee's release after an imprisonment of ten months in Fort Pulaski, near Savannah, Georgia. A copy of a letter from Ulysses S. Grant to President Andrew Johnson, dated March 22, 1866, appeared in the *Fernandina Courier* on May 9, 1866. Grant wrote to President Johnson: "No good will be accomplished by his [Yulee's] confinement." Yulee was released forthwith. Grant's generous gesture toward Yulee gained him the good will of the people of Florida.

The railroad on Amelia Island, successfully resurrected under David Yulee's genius became the focal point, once again, of the island's well being and prosperity. Economic reconstruction under Yulee's leadership came with relative swiftness; reconciliation between Confederates and

Northerners, and between race and race, unfortunately moved at a slower, more grudging, and dilatory pace.

When "repentant" Confederates were allowed to vote again, the polls were rife with fraud on both sides of the political coin. Ballot boxes were stuffed; votes were bought with a drink of whiskey; black voters were given ominous warnings to "vote right." In Nassau County, a candidate bragged that a contrived ruckus in the country road outside the polls distracted the poll-keepers long enough to give his henchmen time to stuff the ballot box. Although women of Amelia Island were not granted suffrage until 1919, a comment in the *Florida Mirror* on November 13, 1880, credited Amelia Island's women for "controlling the votes by controlling the voters."

Political sparring remained the order of the day for years after the war. An amusing illustration is found in a story told by Mr. Herbert Williams, scion of the prominent Marcellus Williams family. Then an old man, Mr. Williams returned to Fernandina in 1948 for a visit to his boyhood home and recalled a family story of a political incident that took place in 1876 in a small downtown city park. Former Confederate General Joseph Finegan was making a vigorous anti-Republican speech from the bandstand, which his opponents, the night before, had sabotaged by sawing nearly through the support structure. In the midst of the General's fiery Democratic speech, the bandstand collapsed. Undaunted, the old soldier picked himself up from the pile of splintered lumber and proclaimed, "The Republican Party will collapse just like this."

The *Florida Mirror*, one of the most valuable historical resources of Fernandina's Golden Age, was a weekly newspaper published from 1878 to 1901. Founded by David Yulee to serve his efforts to expand the railroad that he had started before the war, the *Mirror* became a seductive and persuasive voice in postwar reconstruction and in the ongoing development of Amelia Island and indeed in the state of Florida. The first issue of the *Mirror,* dated November 30, 1878, listed A. B. Campbell and George Burnside as publishers. A year later, George Fairbanks, eminent Florida historian, became its influential editor, serving from 1879 to 1885.

The pages of the *Florida Mirror* reflected the remarkable vitality that prevailed on Amelia Island after the war, as citizens worked together to build a lovely port city of homes, churches, and schools, under-girded by the industries of railroads, shipping, agriculture, tourism, lumber and naval stores, phosphate mining, and all the supporting businesses and professions of a bustling town. A letter to the editor of the *Florida Mirror* from the *Brunswick Appeal,* published January 28, 1880, reflects a colleague's respect: "It is impossible to tell who edits the Fernandina *Florida Mirror,* but it is one of the brightest and best conducted little beauties that visits our sanctum." Fairbanks rarely, if ever, gave himself credit for editorials, articles, and comments published in the *Mirror.* It is impossible to determine his exact participation and responsibility, but this writer gives him personal credit for most of the newspaper's printed content during the years of his editorship.

The pages of the *Mirror* also reflect the raw, biased, unyielding political climate of the post-war era. George R. Fairbanks obviously used his editorial privilege to point out what he believed to be the shortcomings of the Republican candidates for political office in the city, state, and nation. An example of this may be found in the tantalizing bits and pieces of copy which may be read in the *Florida Mirror* between the years 1880 and 1884 relating to the turbulent career of C. A. Haley, Republican mayor of Fernandina. While running for office, Mayor Haley became the subject of personally humiliating letters to the editor and insulting editorial comment. For instance, the *Mirror* published a letter from "A Voter," who wrote: "Never have we been cursed with so complete a specimen of the carpetbagger as the present Republican nominee for Mayor." The "Voter" urged the mayoral candidate to "Pack his carpetbag and go home" (*Florida Mirror*, Mar. 3, 1880). Editor Fairbanks called the "ticket" that had put Haley into Republican nomination "an insult to common sense." Notwithstanding Fairbanks' antipathy to the nomination of carpetbagger Haley, he was elected mayor, albeit "unsatisfactorily to a large body of citizens." Editor Fairbanks commented tersely after Haley's election, "We shall hope for the best."

Three months after Haley was elected mayor by a "meager majority of nine," a "Notice of Foreclosure" appeared in the *Mirror* on July 17, 1880. Haley's property was to be sold on the courthouse steps. Over a hundred years later, one may only guess at the circumstances that brought Haley to such dire straits, but, in subsequent issues of the newspaper, a reader may piece together the intriguing story of a public servant, duly elected mayor of Fernandina, justly or unjustly targeted to receive a full quiver of poison arrows shot by dissatisfied constituents. By hook or crook, on the pages of the *Mirror*, Democrats appeared determined to oust Republican Mayor Haley. On April 2, 1881, the headlines of the *Florida Mirror* proclaimed "The City Government Disbanded." Haley was out. The editor explained, "on going to press," that it had been learned that the Democratic Governor of Florida, William D. Bloxham, had dissolved the "Corporation of the City of Fernandina" and appointed Mayor Gustav Stark and a new slate of aldermen.

The summary ouster of Mayor Haley by Democratic Governor Bloxham, without question, outraged Republicans. The deed was done, however, and City Attorney H. J. Baker rendered his opinion that any question that the governor's newly appointed mayor and aldermen were *de facto* officers of the city "we have thought too plain for controversy" (*Florida Mirror*, Apr. 16, 1881). The controversy, however, led Haley straight to the Supreme Court of Florida where he was vindicated.

Although the highest court in the state had returned Haley to his position as mayor of Fernandina, he continued to be a target of the *Mirror's* editorial barbs and arrows. On November 19, 1881, the editor self-righteously stated: "We have hitherto refrained from any adverse criticism of the City Council." There followed, however, an editorial diatribe protesting the indebtedness of the city and a vehement protest of an ordinance raising the mayor's yearly salary from $200 to $900.

The *Florida Mirror* on November 26, 1881, printed "A Tax Payer's Plaint" defending Haley on its editorial page: "A tax payer asks us to insert a communication charging each of our city papers with vilifying, in the worst possible manner, the Mayor [Haley] and Council." The editor replied: "No vilifying has been done...criticism [has been] decorous...." According to the *Mirror* of January 28, 1882, the ordinance increasing the mayor's salary was overturned and his yearly salary was set at $400. Evidently, the mayor's salary remained a bone of contention for months. The *Mirror* asked editorially on April 1, 1882, whether citizens wished a "nine hundred dollar mayor and a large city debt" or would they elect "able men who will manage the affairs of the city?"

The tribulations relating to Haley's ouster from office reached what must have been, at least to Haley, a satisfactory denouement when the Florida Supreme Court ordered the City of Fernandina to pay the legal fees incurred when he fought to maintain his office as the legitimately elected mayor of Fernandina. A final, plaintive statement in the *Mirror* seemed to summarize the Haley saga: "Putting all these lawyer fees and retainers together, the bill has been a heavy one." In spite of the *Mirror's* unrelenting hostility, Haley won the election for a third term as mayor of Fernandina (*Florida Mirror*, Apr. 7, 1883).

Fair or foul, C. A. Haley stood squarely in the middle of political strife between Democrats and Republicans in the highly charged atmosphere of the time. In the *Florida Mirror*, Republicans received short shrift, and political sparring continued to garner a full share of newsprint. An editorial copied from a Savannah newspaper and published in the *Mirror* on March 31, 1883, declared the Grand Old Party to be "associated with tyranny, spoliation, persecution, shameless rascality, and can never be made respectable." A reporter from the *Mirror* described a Republican mass meeting at the Lyceum Hall as the "lamest one ever held here by Republicans." The Republican speaker from out of town was described as "an overrated stump speaker with no personal magnetism nor eloquence." Applause for the [Republican] speakers was "weak-kneed," and the *Mirror* ungraciously reported that one of the Republican luminaries on the speaker's platform "went to sleep" (*Florida Mirror*, Aug. 23, 1884).

In 1884, when Grover Cleveland was elected president, island Democrats rejoiced. The *Mirror* displayed the large headline: "Florida Democratic." It reported on a torch-lit parade on the streets of Fernandina celebrating Cleveland's election in the November 22, 1884, edition. A booming presidential salute fired by brilliantly uniformed local militia heralded the celebration. The Island City Brass Band led the jubilant crowd through the downtown parade route. Private houses and businesses were brightly illuminated, and bonfires were lighted at intersections of the streets. Marchers carried a large portrait of Cleveland and placards that exclaimed:

In spite of the political flames fanned by the *Mirror,* prosperity came swiftly to Amelia Island after the devastating war. Whether there was true reconciliation between men and races, even today, remains a question without answer. Reconciled or not, island men and women somehow worked

VICTORY WITH HONOR
EQUAL RIGHTS TO BOTH RACES
BURY THE BLOODY SHIRT
OUR COUNTRY - NO NORTH SOUTH EAST OR WEST
FREE SCHOOLS FOR ALL
PROTECTION FOR ALL CLASSES
WE HAVE TURNED THE RASCALS OUT; WE WILL
KEEP THE RASCALS OUT
THE TEMPLE OF LIBERTY
NO LONGER A DEN OF THIEVES
TRUTH CRUSHED WILL RISE AGAIN
WE HAVE RIZ
GOOD WILL TO ALL

together above the vicissitudes of political and social turmoil left behind by civil war. Rebel and Yank worked side by side in the railroad shops; a Federal soldier made a $5 donation to a local Confederate cause (*Florida Mirror*, Apr. 18, 1884); Confederate General and Union Major knelt together in St. Peter's Church; the southern belle married the young gentleman from the North; and the carpetbagger became the town's most respected merchant. The age of reconciliation on Amelia Island was moving toward its Golden Age.

Business Opportunities

Growing Economy

Fine Homes

PROSPERITY

I sland citizens, once combatants on the field of battle, now jousted on the field of politics; but in the market place, they began to set aside their differences and joined forces to build a community alive with promise. As the wounds of war were healing, David Yulee's Florida Railroad was the economic driver of Amelia Island's sprint from reconciliation to prosperity. Not merely a transportation center, Fernandina was hailed as "the Newport of the South" after the railroad in 1877 built the first luxury hotel in Florida for winter visitors, the resplendent Egmont (e. g. *Florida Mirror,* Apr. 12, 1884*).* Together the Florida Railroad and the Egmont launched Fernandina's "Golden Age," as the period of the late nineteenth and early twentieth centuries is known to local historians.

The epic story of the businesses that participated in this dynamic era of Amelia Island's Golden Age is written across the pages of the *Florida Mirror* between the years 1878 and 1900. In this esteemed local newspaper, one may read the shipping statistics of sail and steamer and their manifests of goods and commodities brought in and shipped from the port of Fernandina. Advertisements posted schedules of trains, steamers, and river boats and bore promise of travel from Fernandina to places near and far—St. Marys, Cedar Key, Brunswick, Savannah, New York, Havana, Nassau, Hamburg, and Liverpool. Round trip passage to New York on a Mallory steamer, meals included, cost $45. A round trip ticket to Havana was $26, and a "limited number" of passengers could sail round trip on the *Palma* to the United Kingdom and Mediterranean ports as she delivered her cargo of cotton, naval stores, and lumber. Enticing advertisements displayed in the *Mirror* covered a wide spectrum from professional services, food, shelter, clothing, and coffins, to land offered for sale at $1.50 per acre along the route of Yulee's railroad from Fernandina to Cedar Key. The railroad offered new settlers free passage for "their families and personal effects" (*Florida Mirror*, Jan. 21, 1882).

A clear impression of the prosperity of the Golden Age is found in the very first issue of the *Florida Mirror* on November 30, 1878. The inaugural paper described Fernandina as "the once deserted indigo plantation of the dowager Countess of Egmont. But now there is a change. The old plantation is covered with houses. From the once deserted shore, long wharves with large warehouses project; there are piles of lumber at the wharves of the sawmills destined to be distributed among many foreign nations." These "piles of lumber" included cross ties, hardwood, shingles, and cedar hewed for pencils. In addition, naval stores, cotton, and, later, phosphate were major products exported from the busy docks. Outgoing ships loaded with Florida's bounty glided past newly abandoned Fort Clinch, while the graceful Amelia Light House, constructed from 1838-39, guided returning ships into the harbor. At the peak of Fernandina's prosperity, foreign counsels flying flags of fourteen countries had their headquarters in the port to expedite trade with Europe, the Caribbean, and South America.

A "Winter Pilgrim" from Chicago, in a letter published in the *Florida Mirror* on January 25, 1879, described the growing and prosperous town of Fernandina: "Beautiful homes are being built along shell-paved streets....The houses have pretty grass lawns and flower gardens....Few cities in the South can show more attractive residences." Most of Fernandina's downtown buildings and adjoining blocks of fine residences were built during the Golden Age years from the end of the Civil War through their last glimmer in the first years of the twentieth century. Today, this treasure-trove of structures is one of the largest and richest historic districts to be listed on the National Register of Historic Places.

With the growth of "New Fernandina," the Spanish-platted town of "Old Fernandina" across the marsh to the north soon became known as Old Town. There, in a peaceful riverfront setting, Old Town residents went about their lives as harbor pilots, fishermen, boat builders, shop owners, sawmill operators, and keepers of the quarantine station and government marine facilities. During the building of the jetties in the 1880s, they worked on the barges delivering granite.

Filling the river were Carnegie yachts from Cumberland Island, fishing boats, river tugs, Mallory and Cunard steamers, naptha launches, pilot boats, sailing vessels, and ships from all over the world. On shore were several large sawmills, a railroad shop and foundry, a palmetto fiber factory, barber shops, bakeries, banks, boarding houses, drugstores, a photography studio, saloons, shops, stores, homes, schools, a convent, and churches—a lovely, bustling Victorian town.

The social life of Golden Age citizenry was incredibly diverse. There was a Bath Club at the foot of Broome Street for swimming in the river. A trolley transported tourists and residents from river to ocean. On the shore of the Atlantic Ocean, the Strathmore Hotel, the Atlantic Pavilion, bathhouses, a skeet club, horse races, and a skating rink offered beach activities. Golden Age tourists came by ship and train for winter sojourns in Amelia Island's fine hotels and inns.

The Lyceum Hall, located on the south side of Centre Street between Sixth and Seventh, afforded both tourists and residents an amazing variety of entertainment. Local fraternal meetings, clubs, dances, parties, and even city and county courts were accommodated within its walls. On the Lyceum stage, professional touring groups of singers and actors performed the same operas, plays, and musicals that tourists could enjoy at home in much larger cities.

Golden Age baseball was king of sports: in 1894, Fernandina won the title "Champions of Florida." Tennis was also popular on courts at the Williams and Yulee houses. Sailboat and rowing races took place on the river and "Amelia Beach" hosted horse racing. Fernandinians celebrated May Day annually with a parade and Maypole festivities around the pool in Central Park, which the *Mirror* called a place with "proper shade and shelter set aside with great wisdom and forecast for pleasure and recreation" by the founding city fathers (*Florida Mirror*, June 7, 1884).

Both public and private schools during the Golden Age brought creditable education to children and young people of the island. Bids were let in 1875 for four public schools planned for the island, and schools for both black and white children were soon built. In 1896, a new public school serving white children in all grades opened at Ninth and Centre Street. The public school for black children was located across the street to the north.

Young girls from Maine to Florida attended Saint Mary's Priory, a private Episcopal boarding school located in the antebellum mansion built by General Joseph Finegan. After its Reconstruction service as Chloe Merrick's orphanage, Saint Mary's Priory served the daughters of the eastern elite, including a future Carnegie bride who later persuaded her husband to rebuild the famous Dungeness mansion on neighboring Cumberland Island.

Local and boarding students attended an elegant convent school built in 1882 by the Catholic Sisters of Saint Joseph.

Sister Noelie, an accomplished and aristocratic French nun who had come to the convent from the motherhouse of the Sisters in Le Puy, France, taught convent students piano and violin.

Improved city services became commonplace. *The Florida Mirror*, on September 6, 1879, reported "The city cemetery mapped out" and, three years later, announced "a cemetery association" (*Florida Mirror*, Mar. 4, 1882), although Bosque Bello, Fernandina's major cemetery adjacent to Old Town, contains graves dating back to the Spanish period.

Several volunteer fire fighting companies served the town and responded to fires with good will, horse-drawn water tanks, ladders and buckets. The city boasted a waterworks system in 1883, and the Fernandina Brush and Light Company (brushes were a part of a generator) placed streetlights on the waterfront, Centre Street, North Sixth, and South Seventh Street. For $1.00 per month for businesses or $1.50 for residences, commercial establishments or homes could burn one light bulb per month from 6 p.m. until midnight. Saloons, however, got a bargain rate: $.65 per bulb (*Florida Mirror*, Mar. 24, 1883).

The town of Fernandina made its first baby steps toward cyberspace, when, in 1883, a telephone system was installed. The *Florida Mirror* of March 3, 1883, listed the original subscribers as the Railroad Shops, Capt. D. E. Maxwell, Col. J. C. Read, Fred Hoyt & Co., W. B. C. Duryee, H. E. Dotterer, the Florida Town Improvement Co., Tourist Hotel, McGinnis and Rawson, Mode Bros., C. H. Huot, and J. J. Acosta.

Even in the most prosperous years of the Golden Age, however, city fathers were good managers determined to reduce city expenses. To accomplish one reduction, the chairman of the city's finance committee, Mr. G. F. Avery, proposed the discharge of "one Old Town policeman" and "one from New Town" (*Florida Mirror*, Oct. 20, 1883). Further, he recommended that, instead of renting a horse and cart for the city's scavenger service, the city should buy its own. Two weeks later a public notice appeared in the *Mirror* that the city's horse and cart would be sold to the highest bidder at the corner of Centre and Second Streets with "city script accepted as payment" (*Florida Mirror,* Nov. 3, 1883). Horse and cart were sold at auction, with a loss to the city of $15. So much for reducing the city's expenses.

Finance chairman Mr. Avery, however, had another ace up his sleeve. Mr. Avery pontificated, "I have long been of the opinion, and have at various times urged, that the city have no paupers." State statutes, according to Mr. Avery, "provide that the *County Commission* shall provide for paupers, imbeciles, lunatics, etc., and when that is done there is no need for the *City Council* making any provision for them." Therefore, Mr. Avery suggested, "Place that portion of the expenses where it belongs..." (*Florida Mirror,* Nov. 3, 1883). Subsequent issues of the *Mirror* reveal nothing further on the subject of paupers.

If saving taxpayer's dollars was an eternal theme in city government, so too was touting economic development. The *Mirror's* account of events celebrating the opening of the rail line from Fernandina to Jacksonville reveals most clearly the true spirit of the economic prosperity of the Golden Age. Several articles concerning this important occasion make it easy for the reader to envision the jubilation of the island community at finding itself in easy access by train to the growing city of Jacksonville. According to accounts in the April 9 and April 16, 1881, issues of the *Mirror,* the Short Line, as it was called, from Fernandina to Jacksonville was formally opened on April 6, 1881, and "Nature favored the day."

A thirty-eight gun salute from the Nassau Light Infantry ushered in the celebration with a volley that "thundered out a deep-toned welcome, while steamers and mills almost burst their whistles trying to outdo the howitzers....As if by magic, flags, pennants, and ensigns fluttered in the breeze on all vessels in the harbor....Places of business were closed. The day was a holiday." Eight first-class coaches filled with dignitaries arrived from Jacksonville. Militia groups in handsome uniforms from Savannah and Gainesville joined the local Nassau Light Artillery to add color and glamour to the scene. Yachts from Savannah, Brunswick, Jacksonville, and Saint Augustine competed in a regatta for "fat purses." There were mule and donkey races, sack and hurdle races, wheelbarrow races, a greased pole, and excursions to the beach "by all who could obtain conveyance....All vehicles of the city were called into requisition to take visitors to ride on the magnificent sea beach of Amelia." The writer of the newspaper article "regretted not having a street railroad"—but that would come later.

The gala celebration continued throughout the day and at eight o'clock, there were fireworks—"a magnificent pyrotechnic display [that had been] ordered from New York" (*Florida Mirror*, Mar. 12, 1881). In the river, "the beautiful bark *Imogene* was decorated with Chinese lanterns from her bowsprit to her sternpost. She looked like a fairy ship on a silver sea." The Lyceum was decorated with flags of all nations. "Fernandina and Jacksonville are joined together now with iron bands—these cities by the sea" exulted the *Mirror*. The celebration concluded with a *"grand feu de joie."* At the Egmont Hotel, a ball "thronged with fair women and brave men, pleasantly closed the day."

In its prosperity and charm, the town of Fernandina was handed down to future generations in exquisite detail in the widely-reproduced 1884 *Bird's Eye View Map*. With great perception, on January 5, 1884, the *Mirror* predicted "To our children, [the map] will be a valuable relic in future years." Mr. H. Wellge, a German artist for the publishing house of J. J. Stoner, of Madison, Wisconsin, sketched "every building perfectly [so that] every citizen can point out his own home....The point of observation is 1/2 mile in the air over Amelia Island....Subscriptions are $4.50 per single copy." Mr. Wellge's beautiful map shows the town from river to ocean, with Old Town, Fort Clinch, and Amelia Light in the distance. Railroad and wharves line the river filled with small craft and vessels of steam and sail. Inset drawings on the map depict Tiger Island, "Second Street Looking North West," and a delightful drawing of the Strathmore Hotel at the beach, with bathers frolicking in the surf and beach cottages and bathhouses close by. The largest inset is that of the elegant Egmont Hotel. According to the *Mirror*, the town was "captured in perfect outline, as if seen by a bird soaring one half mile above the island."

During her Golden Age, not all of Amelia Island's prosperity came from the business pursuits of law-abiding citizens. For several years before the outbreak of the Spanish American War in 1898, Amelia Island responded with enthusiasm and blatantly unlawful action to aid Cuba in its effort to wrest itself from Spanish rule. The very real desire of Floridians to aid the Cubans was sparked as much by the profitability of arms shipped surreptitiously out of Fernandina to Cuban patriots as by genuine concern for the oppressed Cubans seeking democracy. Jośe Marti, adored hero of Cuba's fight for independence, enjoyed the hospitality of the Florida House for a week in 1893 while he supervised an attempt to ship armaments and supplies to Cuban rebels on fast yachts out of Fernandina.

In 1900, Fernandina's harbor was still a busy port. Ships sailed away loaded with lumber, naval stores, and phosphate bound for the industrial North, Europe, Nassau, Barbados, and Martinique, but Fernandina was gradually losing her title of Florida's busiest port to the cities of Tampa and Jacksonville. The expansion of railroads into central and southern Florida by Henry Plant and Henry Flagler gave tourists access to warmer and more exotic places than Amelia Island and her aging hotels. The island's deep natural harbor was no longer its economic trump card.

While Tampa and Jacksonville boomed, the Golden Age of Amelia Island began to fade with the century into a quieter, less prosperous pace. The physical essence, however, of that remarkable period of Amelia Island history lives on in Fernandina's downtown buildings and adjoining residential blocks. Through these buildings and landmarks a precious heritage has been passed to the citizens and visitors of Amelia Island, a fragile heritage that deserves to be nurtured, cherished, and carefully guarded. The chapters that follow form a compendium of some of our Golden Age institutions, industries, social activities, and landmark events, the seeds of which, kept briefly covered by the ashes of Civil War and its aftermath, sprouted and blossomed on Amelia Island for half a century.

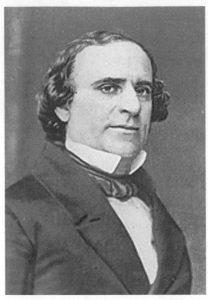

David Yulee was born at St. Thomas, West Indies in 1810. He studied law and practiced at St. Augustine. He served as a Democrat in the Florida Senate (Florida's first Senator) until the outbreak of Civil War in 1861. He founded and established the Florida Railroad at Fernandina and became known as the "Father of Florida Railroads."

AIMH

Rails ran from Fernandina docks to the passenger depot at the foot of Centre Street then across the Florida peninsula to docks at Cedar Key.

AIMH

Making a Living
The Railroad

The first cross-state railroad in Florida was born in "New Fernandina" and at birth became the cornerstone of the island economy. Opened from Amelia Island to Cedar Key in March 1861, the new Florida Railroad's bright future was soon extinguished by a war that had literally usurped its tracks and engines and imprisoned David Levy Yulee, its founder and guide. After ten months in Fort Pulaski prison following the Civil War, Yulee received a presidential pardon, thanks in large part to the intervention of General Grant. He returned to the devastated town of Fernandina and began the task of regaining control of his railroad and rebuilding its war-ruined tracks, bridges, and docks from Fernandina to the Gulf. By 1866, trains were finally able to reach Gainesville, and by 1869, the Florida Railroad was once again in service.

Yulee's genius brought trains from across the state to Fernandina loaded with the bounty of Florida citrus, strawberries, vegetables, cotton, cedar, and phosphate. Yulee's connections and gift for publicity also led widespread shipping lines, including the famous Mallory Line, to stop at Fernandina's deepwater port and connect with his "Atlantic, Gulf and West India Transit Company," as the Florida Railroad was known by 1872. By 1886, connections were even available from the Egmont Hotel to the beach on two miles of track of the Fernandina and Amelia Beach Railway. Through his railroad, Yulee led Fernandina into its Golden Age.

Busy railroad shops, located on the riverfront at Date and Elm Streets supported the revived and thriving railroad. These shops included foundries and machine, carpenter, paint, and upholstery shops, providing a major source of employment for many citizens, black and white. Their activities included tasks such as "building 40 new boxcars with "Mr. Hernandez as supervisor," as the *Florida Mirror* reported February 12, 1881.

Former resident Miss Marie Cone was nearing one hundred years old in 1989 when she recalled that "dinner boys," just before noon, would go to the homes of the men who worked at the railroad shops to pick up pails containing hot lunches for the workers. The dinner boy would slip the handle of the pail on a long pole carried across his shoulders. He would then go to the next house, to another, and another, until his pole, on each side, tinkled an octave or more of tin pails ready to be opened by hungry railroad workers at the sound of the noon whistle.

The only known photograph of Fernandina's rail yard before the 1898 hurricane laid waste to most of the railroad's resources.

Collection of Jan H. Johannes

AIMH

*The old railroad depot had been destroyed by the hurricane of
1898, as had many of the buildings of downtown Fernandina.*

On April 6, 1881, Fernandina had a gala celebration
to mark the completion of the "Short Line," officially the
Fernandina and Jacksonville Railroad, connecting the town
to Jacksonville. In retrospect, the festivities were ironic:
Jacksonville was on its way to replacing Fernandina as
northeast Florida's transportation hub and it soon became
clear that the railroad link was not to be a marriage of equals.
In July of that year, Yulee surrendered control of his railroad
to British investor Sir Edward J. Reed and retired from active
management. He left the town he had brought to prosperity
and moved to Washington D.C., where he died on October
10, 1886. By the time of Yulee's death, Henry Flagler had
developed plans for the opulent Ponce de Leon Hotel in
St. Augustine, the first in a series of lavish hotels along his
Florida East Coast Railway that by-passed the increasingly
shabby "Newport of the South" and soon lured Fernandina's

Golden Age tourists to more up-to-date luxurious hotels in balmier locales.

By 1900, Fernandina's railroad had had its place in the sun. In 1898, the railroad depot and shops were casualties of the 100 mph winds and 14 foot tidal surge of the hurricane that struck just to the north of Fernandina on October 2. The railroad moved quickly to rebuild the depot, described as "one of the nicest structures in the South" by the Florida *Times Union* on May 28, 1899. Nevertheless, other Florida railroad lines that by-passed Fernandina increasingly bore the products of Florida's groves, mines, farms, and forests to ports able to handle more rail traffic than Amelia Island, with its limited bridge access, could accommodate. The momentum of the busy railroad shops slowed considerably. By 1926, they were completely closed.

AIMH

The Fernandina depot is just out of site beyond the two story fish market. This transportation hub of 1870 to 1920s mixed trolleys, freight and passenger trains and horse and buggies with ocean-going steamers.

Making a Living
The Port

In a letter published in the *Florida Mirror* on January 16, 1879, David Yulee described freight awaiting shipment from the port of Fernandina to "Savannah, Charleston, New York and Europe."

"Eight thousand barrels of rosin lined the railroad and covered the docks. Cotton and cottonseed are piled high on Centre Street dock for lack of space at other wharves. Any ordinary businessman can calculate for himself what all this portends. Florida is exporting largely, the result will be wealth."

Yulee's words are as clear as a photograph of Fernandina's busy Golden Age riverfront.

On November 30, 1879, the *Mirror* reported that "24 steamers per week, including two regular steamships from New York, could be seen in Fernandina waters." On December 13, 1879, the *Mirror* asked, "Has the average Fernandinian comprehended that we have two foreign steamship lines?"

From Fernandina's bustling wharves laden with bounty from the Florida's forests, farms, and seas, the steamer *Palmer*, owned by the Fernandina and United Kingdom Line organized by William Lawtey, made regular voyages to Europe. The *Palmer* was described as "250 feet long, 33 foot beam, 1171 tons register....with unsurpassed accommodations for passengers." Her commander, Captain Benjamin B. Murrell, was proclaimed a "genial, well-souled man." (*Florida Mirror,* Nov. 30, 1878)

The Mallory Steamship Line's Florida steamers included the *Western Texas*, the *City of Austin*, and the *City of Dallas*. "The *City of Dallas* will leave Fernandina every Friday for New York and from New York Pier 20, East River, every Friday for Fernandina, to suit the tide" (*Florida Mirror*, Dec. 13, 1879). The Mallory fleet also included the *City of San Antonio*, the *State of Texas*, and the *Carondelet*. The *Western Texas* made regular trips from Fernandina to Havana and Nassau.

The *Mirror* reported that the *Western Texas* "has been built up. New houses on deck and other improvements...enable her to accommodate 76 first class passengers. Excursion tickets are being sold, good until October 1st, for $30 for the trip from Fernandina to New York and return" (*Florida Mirror* Aug. 23, 1879). The *Mirror* boasted that Fernandina was the only harbor in Florida having a line of steamers to New York or Liverpool, England, and the only port to have a line of steamers to Nassau, Bahamas (*Florida Mirror*, Mar. 11, 1882).

The newspaper noted other foreign trade that kept fourteen foreign counsels busy: "The Barque *Palo Alto*.... is now loading with railroad ties for Natal, Brazil. She will take about 25,000 ties....The brig, *Captain Penton*, direct from Liverpool, arrived Thursday, 48 days out....Cargo, 3662 bags salt, 157 bundles hoop iron, and 10 tons English channel coal" (*Florida Mirror*, Nov. 26, 1878).

Cotton and cottonseed were important commodities shipped out of Fernandina's port. "The most valuable shipment ever made from this port" consisted of "27,000 sacks of cotton seed, 380 bales of Sea Island cotton, and 81 bags of short cotton." The sound of congratulatory bells and whistles from "every steamer in the port and all the mills on shore," was heard as the British steamer *Kaieteur*, bound for Liverpool, headed out to sea with this prize cargo (*Florida Mirror*, Dec. 13, 1879).

The Borden docks were at the foot of Dade Street and North Front Street. The lumber docks below ran from near Centre Street north, almost to Old Town. Dozens of three, four and five masted schooners were constantly loading lumber and railroad ties.

AIMH

Naval stores or resin arrived at the harbor by rail and river boats before being loaded in the cargo holds of large ocean-going steamers enroute to the north and Europe. The city dock at the foot of Centre Street (below) is shown busy with the steamer Hildegarde, a launch from Cumberland Island and an unidentified river steamer.

AIMH

The quotation from the *Mirror* of March 22, 1884, is typical of many that published that described cargoes shipped out of the port of Fernandina during her Golden Age: "The *State of Texas* left with 40 passengers, 400 logs of cedar, 477 cases cedar, 300 barrels rosin, 20 packages vegetables, 53 cans of shrimp, 16 boxes oranges, 96 packages merchandise, and 2 refrigerated boxes strawberries." The article also noted that fish dealers shipped shad in "large quantities to the north."

Even an occasional whaler may have been seen in the colorful and busy port of Fernandina: "Seven whales taken since February last between Fernandina and St Helena's.....500 barrels of oil were produced" (*Florida Mirror*, Apr. 10, 1880).

A copy of a letter written to the editor of the Springfield, Massachusetts, *Republican* appeared in the shipping news reported by the *Florida Mirror* on March 8, 1879. The letter described the writer's visit to one of Fernandina's busy Golden Age docks. As the man lay in his bunk aboard a steamer that was unloading its cargo he was "kept awake all night by the noise of the unloading of goods...but all night long I was delighted with the sweet perfume of Florida flowers wafted in my open window by gentle zephyrs. On awakening in the morning, I found they were unloading guano" (*Florida Mirror*, Mar. 8, 1879). Sweetish smelling guano, actually the droppings of sea birds, was a commonly-used agricultural fertilizer.

For the black longshoremen, on whose backs the success of the port depended, all was not sweet, however. The *Florida Mirror*, of June 30, 1883, reported: "Colored laboring men of the city have formed an organization to be known as Fernandina Labor Society. The organization was for "the mutual protection of laboring men..., principally dock workers who propose to demand $1.75 per day."

Shipping in Fernandina suffered a major setback in 1888 when the black longshoremen finally went on strike. Alice Youngblood, Amelia Island's noted Florida Writers' Project historian, wrote of the dramatic beginning of the strike: "An unknown Negro, who came into town on a large white horse, organized a strike, raising a flag and gathering crowds by his exhortations." The port of Fernandina was paralyzed. Local authorities, fearing looming economic disaster, summoned troops from Gainesville to assist in bringing order. The strike only ended when a severe outbreak of yellow fever diverted black strikers and outraged white citizens from the brink of violent confrontation.

Sailing ships and steamers carrying cargo were not the only vessels in Amelia Island waters during the Golden Age. Comfortable riverboats bearing supplies, mail, and passengers plied daily and weekly routes to towns up the St. Marys River to Brunswick and Savannah. Familiar riverboats were the *Hildegarde*, the *Harry Lee*, the *City of Bridgeton,* the *Flora,* and the *Florence*. Strong work boats and river tugs bearing the names *Dandy, Wade Hampton, Gladiator, Dauntless, Commodore*, and *Three Friends* pushed and tugged huge rafts of logs to sawmills and pushed lighters loaded with barrels of turpentine and rosin to Fernandina docks. These boats supported pile drivers and dredges and, in the 1890s, were known to deliver machetes and rifles to Cuban freedom fighters. Vessels of the harbor pilots and many fishing boats added their particular charm to the waterfront scene.

Through the years, the captains and officers of the regularly scheduled ships became valued friends of the St. Marys River families of lumber and naval stores producers and the families of pilots, shipping agents, factors, and merchants. Friendly ship captains occasionally invited fortunate young people to sail away in their care to Martinique, Barbados, or wherever the ship delivered North Florida's lumber and naval stores products. New York and Baltimore were other favorite excursions for the young people. In 1902, one of the young men of the Mizell lumber merchant family was aboard a ship bound for the island of Martinique in the care of the ship's captain. As the ship neared the harbor, the air was full of the smoke and fumes of the terrible volcanic eruption of Mont Pelee. Suzanne Hardee proudly displayed a bowl from the ruined city, originally full of volcanic ash, in her china cabinet.

The success of the port depended upon that of the railroad, and as the railroad's importance diminished in comparison to growing transportation centers in Jacksonville and Tampa, shipping declined as well. As World War I

This image takes one back to the 19th century when schooners, brigs, brigantines, and barks entered the harbor and loaded railroad ties, lumber, naval stores, and all types of non-perishables for delivery around the world. Before loading, most ships dropped their ballast to the harbor's floor where it remains today.

AIMH

Schooner Dock loaded with Yellow Pine. FERNANDINA, Fla.

approached, shipping vessels from far-off ports yielded their places on the Fernandina docks to shrimpers and fishing boats. Pogy [menhaden] fishermen unloaded their catches at a processing plant at the mouth of Egans Creek, and a phosphate elevator towered above the fish houses and canneries that lined the waterfront. Only curling photographs remained as mementos of the glory days of Fernandina's deep water port.

Making a Living
The Harbor Pilots

Harbor pilots, sometimes called bar pilots, were a vital, colorful, and prestigious profession during Amelia Island's Golden Age. Captains who had served a vigorous apprenticeship of three to five years in local waters formed a closely-held guild of seamen that licensed newcomers only after a strenuous examination.

In 1837, Captain Samuel Cribb and Captain George W. Latham established the Fernandina Branch Pilots Association. (George Latham was the son of Amos Latham, Revolutionary War veteran and Amelia Island's first lighthouse keeper.) The members of this exclusive association were daring and courageous men whose profession of piloting was as much the warp and woof of Amelia Island's Golden Age as that of railroading. Most of the Fernandina Branch Pilots lived in Old Town, the original Spanish town of Fernandina. S. G. W. Benjamin, a writer for *Harper's New Monthly Magazine,* visited Old Town and, in his article in the November 1878 issue, described the town as "a sleepy hamlet occupied chiefly by pilots."

Pilots and their helpers watched from a tower near Old Town Plaza for the dozens of ships that neared the island bearing the people and products that fed the Golden Age economy. Members of a pilot family tell that the platform of the earliest tower, made of cypress, was almost whittled away by lookouts as they waited tedious hours watching for the hundreds of ships that sailed into Amelia Island waters. In 1902, the pilots purchased an eighty-foot steel tower that had been built on the southeast corner of Estrada and San Fernando Streets for a lookout and survey point when the harbor jetties were being constructed. A lookout stood on the tower to signal work crews when trains were arriving loaded with granite for the jetties and when empty barges returned from the jetty site to be loaded again.

Pilots were kept busy during the Golden Age when ships from New York, Boston, Philadelphia, Baltimore, and European and Latin American countries entered Fernandina's deep harbor to load lumber, naval stores, cotton, and phosphate. When a lookout signaled that a ship was nearing the bar, the pilot, dressed in an immaculately-tailored business suit and fedora, boarded his pilot boat and headed to the open sea. To board the incoming vessel, the pilot was rowed by his crew in a longboat to the side of the ship where he made the oftentimes life-threatening leap to a rope ladder by which he boarded the visiting ship. Presenting his credentials, the pilot assumed command of the ship, issuing orders to the helmsman and engine room until the vessel was safely moored at one of Fernandina's many docks. To return the ship to open sea, the dangerous and challenging procedure was reversed.

In the early days of piloting, the business was carried on in longboats and rowboats. For many years, two longboats used by the pilots of Fernandina hung suspended in the sally port of Fort Clinch. These longboats, the *Brilliant Star* and the *Osceola*, were built on Harker's Island, North Carolina. The *Brilliant Star* was painted gray. The *Osceola*, owned by Captain William Jones Davis, was painted gray with a red stripe. Longboats were traditionally named for the first ship piloted into port. A longboat was built for speed and its crew would row many miles out to sea to meet incoming vessels. Rival crews raced to be first to board the ship nearing the bar. A story is told that when one Old Town pilot rushed to his boat after a ship was sighted, he found his boat loaded with ballast rocks by a rival.

Most of the following information and quotations are taken from brief biographical sketches of the pilots of the Fernandina and St Marys Entrance found in *Webb's History of Florida,* 1885, from conversations with Captain George T. Davis, and from the research of Helen Gordon Litrico, noted Fernandina historian:

The Captains James and William Bell were twin brothers, born in 1841 in North Carolina. They were said to look so much alike they could fool everyone, even their wives. James and William Bell are remembered in Fernandina as much for the houses they built as for their reputations as harbor pilots. They built several houses in Fernandina and Old Town. In 1882, James Bell built the most noted of the Bell houses, the Captain's House that faces the Plaza in Old Town. Other houses built by James Bell were the W. A. Mahoney home,

Amelia Now

*One of the
Bell brothers.*

built about 1888, on the southwest corner of Eighth and Cedar Streets; the Mike Salvador cottage, located mid-block between Fourth and Ash Streets; and the O'Hagan house at 121 North Third Street. William Bell built houses on three corners of South Eighth and Beech Streets. The fine old house on the northeast corner, built in 1889, was for decades the residence of members of the Bell family. William Bell also built the Lasserre house at 130 South Seventh Street, now owned by the heirs of Charles and Frieda Nagel Lasserre. The Lasserre house, built about 1903-1905, is located on the

JHJ

Two Old Town homes belonging to harbor pilots of long ago. Above, the Bell brothers' home and below, the home of Captain William Jones Davis, both adjacent to the plaza and close to the river's edge.

AIMH

site of the gardens of the Egmont Hotel. William died in 1915, twelve years after his brother James. They are buried side by side in St. Peter's cemetery.

Captain Samuel Cribb was co-founder of the Fernandina Branch Pilots Association. He began piloting in 1837, having "few equals and no superiors in his trade." Captain David Cribb was the son of Captain Samuel Cribb. He was "said to have been raised on the bar" and "made" in 1866, a term used when one became a licensed pilot. Captain Albin Danburg was a native of Sweden. Captain Robert Downes was born on Cumberland Island in 1856, of English parents. For a number of years he was captain of a riverboat, and, after completing the required apprenticeship, he became a bar pilot in 1882. Captain Downes purchased the Captain James Bell house on the Plaza at Old Town where he and his family lived for many years.

Captain Henry Johnson came to Amelia Island in a United States Navy vessel, served a local apprenticeship, and was made pilot. Captain Thomas Lasserre came to Old Town from Brunswick, Georgia, in 1878, and became a pilot of the St. Andrews branch at the age of 18. Captain George Latham co-founded the original Fernandina Branch Pilots. From 1837, he served continually in this organization until his death in 1876. Captain George Latham, Jr., followed the path of his father's career and was made pilot in 1877, "a man of unquestioned skill in his profession who has brought many a vessel safely over the bar." According to *Pioneers of Florida's First Coast,* Captain N. B. McNeil, a Georgia native, had "few if any superiors" in his profession. He received his license in 1822.

Captain James Morse was a son-in-law of George Latham, co-founder of the Fernandina Branch Pilots. Captain Morse's sons, Edward Francis and James A. Morse, followed in their father's profession. Captain Edward Francis Morse was one of the Harbor Masters of the port of Fernandina. His son Charles was made pilot in 1940. Captain Joseph H. Newton was a pilot from North Carolina who transferred to Amelia Island in association with the Captains Bell. Captain William Sharpe, born in 1819, was a native of England. He came to Fernandina from the state of Maine "during the war." Sharpe served in the Navy during the war with Mexico. He was described in *Webb's History of Florida* as "hale and hearty." All of the above-named pilots lived in Old Town, Fernandina, except for Samuel Cribb, who lived "up the St Marys River." *Webb's* classified them all as "genial, hospitable gentlemen."

The Amelia Island pilots reorganized about 1893 as the Cumberland Sound Pilot Association, with Captain William Jones Davis as president and Captain Thomas Lasserre as secretary. Membership also included James Bell, William Bell, Thomas Smith Davis, Robert Downes, Henry Johnson, George Latham, Jr., N. B. McNeil, Edward Francis Morse, James A. Morse, Joseph N. Newton, and William Sharpe.

An interesting family paper handed down to present descendants of the George Latham family is a legal agreement, dated 1876, between the pilots of the *Excelsior* and the pilots of the *Jenny Lind*, Captain George Latham, Captain William Sharpe, Captain James Morse, Captain Albin Danburg, and Captain David Cribb, commanding and sailing the Pilot Boat *Excelsior*, and Captain James Bell, Captain William Bell and Captain Joseph H. Newton, commanding and sailing the Pilot Boat *Jenny Lind*. The agreement, signed by all the above pilots contains the following:

> Friendly, good and amicable relations should exist between the parties of these presents. Each should not only feel an interest in the welfare of the others, every one should combine and work together to promote

the property of all. Captains and crews of the Pilot Boats shall continue to direct and sail the boats to which they respectively belong with unabated energy, industry, skill, and perseverance and work together in each others interest.

Fees, the agreement specified, were to be divided equally based on net earnings of each boat. Upon the death of a pilot, his widow was to be paid $25 per month for the remainder of her husband's contract. In case of sickness, the pilots would continue to draw pay "as if personally present and at duty." Each pilot duly signed the document.

In addition to the pilot boats *Excelsior* and the *Jenny Lind* mentioned in the above agreement, the Fernandina Branch Pilots owned the *Robert W. Cowan*. The 50-foot 25-ton *Robert W. Cowan* was built in Southport, North Carolina, in 1872. Another pilot boat was the *Agnes Belle*. The *Agnes Belle* was described in the *Florida Mirror* of May 27, 1882, as the "new pilot boat purchased by Pilots Cribb, Latham, Sharpe, and Lasserre." She was built in Portland, Maine, 65 feet in length, 18 1/2 foot beam, 30 tons of burthen, a draft of water 8 feet 9 inches, and schooner rigged. She was rated the "fastest pilot boat on the New England coast." The pilots also owned the 60-foot, 29-ton *Frances Elizabeth,* built in 1879 in Charleston, South Carolina.

One of the first pilot boats was said to be the *Swancy Jack*. According to a story told by a member of the George Latham family to Alice Youngblood during her research for *Seeing Fernandina*, the builder of the *Swancy Jack* was Captain George Latham, co-founder of the Fernandina Branch Pilots. So distinguished a vessel was the *Swancy Jack* that Latham ladies decorated her with finery and lace curtains until she was, so to speak, queen of the St. Marys Entrance. A pirate, said to be handsome—one of the many freebooters who sailed in and out of Fernandina's harbor—was smitten with the beautiful *Swancy Jack* and demanded to buy her. Although Latham had no wish to sell his prized vessel, he was a practical man and knew he had to accept the piratical offer of payment in gold or find himself with neither boat nor bullion. Farewell, *Swancy Jack.*

The brave pilots of Amelia Island waters carried out successful missions often noted in the *Florida Mirror.* For example, a headline in the *Mirror* on October 8, 1881, exclaims: "Bark *Albina* Ashore South of the Bar. A Total Loss, the Crew Saved." Subsequently, a letter addressed to "Messrs Bell Bros., Newton, and Johnson of the pilot boat *Jenny Lind,*" appeared in the *Florida Mirror* on December 17, 1881, and further explained the headline:

Neither the Captain, the writer, nor crew would have been alive to tell the tale for we had been in our boats 15 hours struggling with the breakers and were exhausted 2 miles from shore separated from it by large and angry breakers with sharks for company... After taking us on board the little Jennie the generous offers made to us of dry clothing, invitations to their firesides and more substantial aid was in the mind of the writer considered to be true hospitality and duly appreciated. I desire to say that in my experience the Fernandina pilots are on hand when wanted.

J. C. Norton, late First Officer of the bark *Albina,* signed the document.

All stories in the *Mirror* relating to piloting were not always of successful missions. For example, one may read in the *Mirror* that Mr. C. H. Mallory, senior member of the famous Mallory shipping firm, had come to Fernandina to examine "the condition of the wrecked Mallory steamer, *City of Austin.*" The steamer's regular run was from New York to

Fernandina and from Fernandina to Nassau and Cuba. The *Mirror* described the loss of the vessel as the "most serious that has occurred and appears to be attributable solely to the pilot in charge." The reporter from the *Mirror* further described the *City of Austin* aground on Pelican Shoals "parted amidships" with "seven feet of water in her hold....She now lies with her bow out of water and her stern settled, so that at high water she is covered to the hurricane deck." Forty-five passengers and their baggage were safely transferred to another steamer *(Florida Mirror*, Apr. 30, 1881). On October 8, 1881, the *Mirror* reported "another wreck." The wrecked brig *Puntaluna,* loaded with ballast, was described as 18 years old, 260 tons, and valued at $10,000: "His colors [were] set for a pilot but none boarded him." The wreck, "bought at auction" for $25, was the sad ending of the *Puntaluna.*

The serious, stressful, oftentimes dangerous work of piloting was sometimes alleviated by the pleasure of sailing

Though the harbor is generally of sufficient depth for most sailing vessels, there was the occasional grounding mishap. Here the bark 'Ruby' is assisted by the tug 'Wade Hampton' off of the bar.

AIMH

with friends and family, or indulging in a day of fishing at the famous snapper banks. The *Florida Mirror* of August 12, 1882, describes the pleasure of "a trip to the snapper banks [on the *Jennie Lind*] with a party of young men from the city: "Sam Swann, John A. Edwards, Donie Maxwell, Mart Proctor, John Pope, Dr. Loomis, Ike Mode, John Papy, John Gum, and G. L. Baltzell, Captain Johnson commanding." The writer of the account who signed himself "One of the Party," described the novel method used to locate the snapper banks. A member of the group dropped a soap-coated lead sinker to the ocean floor. When the sinker brought up particles of coral, the vessel was known to be in the correct location for snapper fishing. Fishing was "fast and furious" when the cry was heard, "Sail in sight!" The pilot captain announced that he had to "speak to her...Up anchor and away for the ship which proved to be a bark... we spoke to her and found her, much to our captain's disappointment, bound for Brunswick, Georgia. "About ship," was the next command, and back to the banks where we fished until our hands were blistered....70 snappers, four groupers, 17 black fish."

Periodically, Amelia Island's Golden years were plagued by outbreaks of yellow fever and harbor pilots were constrained to follow the rules and regulations of quarantine set down by the Board of Health of Nassau County. The following notice appeared in the *Florida Mirror* on April 16, 1881: "During the quarantine season, it shall be the duty of all pilots to conduct to the quarantine grounds all vessels arriving in the harbor except the lines of coast-wise steamers." On June 27, 1885, the *Mirror* printed an order to the pilots to bring vessels to anchor at the Quarantine Station in Old Town. All vessels arriving from "infected ports" were required to discharge their ballast across the river at Tiger Island. (For additional information on pilots and yellow fever, see the chapter entitled "Yellow Fever.")

An account of harbor rules and regulations appeared in the *Fernandina Express* on June 18, 1881. The Harbor Master was charged to procure a suitable berth for vessels and to see that they were "properly moored."

Regular scheduled ships shall have preference. Masters of vessels shall not permit ballast, rubbish, or dirt of any kind to be thrown in the river or harbor. Ballast shall be discharged above high water mark. Sweepings of the deck and ashes from the caboose must be carted away. No tar or turpentine may be boiled on the wharf or on the vessel. The Master of the vessel shall brace around the yards, cathead, the anchors and jibboom whenever required by the Harbor Master. No ballast may be landed without permission of the Harbor Master.

Dockage fees for ships in the harbor were "Four cents per foot from taffrail to knighthead."

Update

Among the men who have served as harbor masters of the port of Fernandina in the 20th century were J. Fred Lohman, John Richardson Hardee, George T. Davis, and William Hardee Kavanaugh.

Captain George T. Davis, youngest son of William Jones Davis, served as master pilot and harbor master of Amelia Island waters and St. Marys Entrance for 41 years. Captain Davis and Captain Charles B. Morse, son of Captain Ed Morse, were both fourth generation pilots. They began their apprenticeships together in 1933, and were made full Branch Pilots in 1940. Captain Morse terminated his appointment at the end of World War II. Captain Davis retired in 1979.

Commander William Sweatt, grandson of Captain William Jones Davis, and grand nephew of Captain George T. Davis, continues his family tradition and serves as state pilot for the port of St. Marys and federal pilot of the Trident Submarine base at Kings Bay, Georgia. Commander Sweatt is a graduate of the United States Naval Academy. William Hardee Kavanaugh served his apprenticeship under Captain George T. Davis. Kavanaugh, the current Harbor Master and senior pilot of the port of Fernandina, was the last pilot in the state of Florida to be commissioned under the old apprentice system. At present, the licensing of pilots is authorized under the Florida Department of Professional Regulations.

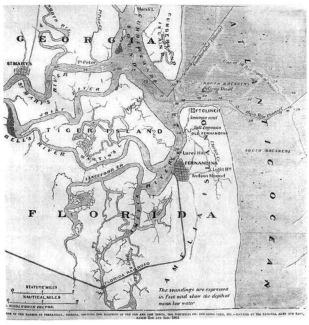

Fernandina Harbor in 1862.

Florida Memory Project
Florida Department of State
RC 04651

Making a Living
The Jetties

Along with the graceful Amelia Light, completed in 1839, the jetties jutting from Fernandina's north beach remain an enduring landmark to Amelia Island's shipping history.

The *Florida Mirror* of December 11, 1878, reported that "a new channel [has] broken through the shoals of the harbor passage." Such occurrences were common at the St. Marys entrance to the harbor when there were no jetties to harness the tide into a predictable channel. Editorial comment began to appear on the pages of the *Mirror* to express the importance of jetties to stabilize and deepen the channel into Fernandina's harbor. David Yulee asked the Fernandina Board of Trade for a survey to demonstrate the need (*Florida Mirror*, Apr. 10 1880).

Statistics "on the Fernandina Bar" provided by "a naval commission" were quoted in the *Mirror* on April 17, 1880: "About 14 feet at low water. A tidal rise of six feet making 20 feet at high tide." According to the *Mirror*, it was imperative to deepen the harbor due to the ever-shifting sands of the St. Marys entrance and the increasing draft of the newer ships coming into port. A jetty system would channel the flow of waters from the St. Marys River and "increase the scouring process" of the channel and improve its depth. In 1880, Congress approved funding for two rock jetties that would extend parallel to each other from the shores of Amelia and Cumberland Island. On August 14, 1880, a notice in the *Mirror* "invited proposals for work on improving

Government House was constructed at Old Town's plaza to facilitate construction of the jetties. Here, Captain Robert Downes poses beside the new addition to old Fernandina's landscape.

AIMH

Cumberland Sound." The proposals were to be addressed to "Lt. Col. Q. A. Gilmore, of U. S. A. Engineers Office, New York, N. Y."

Securing the necessary government funds to undertake the work on the channel was a slow matter. Beginning at $30,000, the appropriation jumped to $350,000. Then, according to the *Mirror* of February 12, 1881, it was cut back to $100,000. Fernandina and Nassau County legislators battled their counterparts from Jacksonville, St. Augustine, and Tampa, all of them fighting for the biggest share of governmental pie. Even after work had begun on the Amelia Island port entrance, the fight continued for funds to keep the project going. Appropriations see-sawed back and forth. An editorial comment in the *Mirror* of May 13, 1882, called it "unjust discrimination" to receive only $50,000 for the Cumberland Island entrance, when $150,000 had been appropriated for the St. Johns River bar. Another editorial on January 27, 1883, complained of "piecemeal appropriations."

When the first funds were finally allocated, the work commenced of laying the "mattresses" on which the jetty rocks would be placed. Lara, Ross and Company held the bid for contracting the project, perhaps hired, in part, because of their offer "to purchase material for their work *here* rather than to import" *(Florida Mirror*, Sept. 25, 1880). The task of harnessing the currents of the sea was a difficult one. "Major Duryee has taken a contract for completing a portion of the Cumberland jetties. The former contractors have failed to pursue the work vigorously" *(Florida Mirror*, Nov. 26, 1881).

On April 30, 1881, the *Mirror* reported that "Lt. Fisk, U. S. Army, in charge of improvement of the Cumberland Sound entrance" had paid an inspection visit. "Contractors have erected a wharf and comfortable quarters for employees...A vessel is due loaded for the laying down of the mattresses.... work will follow the line of Pelican Shoal." "Comfortable quarters" must have been well received by workers who had previously lived in temporary shelters on Cumberland Island.

The foundation mattresses were mats approximately eighty feet in length made of logs and brush. The *Mirror*, on February 11, 1882, reported the plan for the jetties:

> [The plan] consists of two low jetties composed of rip-rap stone resting on a foundation mattress of logs, or logs and brush, starting from the shores on the opposite sides of the entrance and extending seaward across the bar upon lines so directed that the outer ends will be parallel to each other and from 3000 to 3500 feet apart of such distance as may hereafter be adopted....During the present fiscal year it is proposed to continue work on the north jetty and perhaps begin construction of the south jetty.

An average of 22,000 tons of rock, loaded on barges 150 feet wide, was deposited per month (*Fernandina Express,* May 21, 1881). Granite from Georgia and South Carolina arrived constantly, usually by sea. Typical reports on the shipment of the granite can be read in the *Mirror* such as "Three cargoes of stone are now afloat for the jetties. This will finish up the work under the present appropriation" [*Florida Mirror,* Jul. 29, 1882).

In Old Town, government engineers built a steel tower to be used as a survey point for building the jetties. The tower also functioned as a lookout for train cars arriving with loads of granite rock or for empty rock barges returning from the jetty site. Workers could be signaled to get ready for the hard work of loading or unloading the granite. Upon completion of the jetties, the government sold the tower to the harbor pilots based in Old Town.

Nancy Seibert, a long-time resident of Old Town, recalled that a "Government House" stood in Old Town during the construction of the jetties. The engineers, surveyors, and others involved in working on the jetties both lived in and had their offices in the building during the almost twenty years it took to complete the immense project. The "Government House" was torn down in 1922 (Nancy Seibert scrapbook, Amelia Island Museum of History).

A letter to David Yulee from U. S. Engineer Q. A. Gilmore appeared in the *Mirror* on August 16, 1881: "In reply to your communication, I have the honor to say that the low jetties I am constructing at the entrance to Cumberland

This classic photograph was taken from the Old Town lookout tower looking south toward new Fernandina.

AIMH

Sound will, in my opinion, maintain a low water depth of 21 feet....I estimate that the work will be finished in 3 or 4 years." A jetty to protect Fort Clinch "from the encroaching tide" was being constructed at the same time as the north and south jetties. (*Florida Mirror*, Apr. 16, 1881).

The people of Fernandina were complimented on their harbor improvements in an article printed in the *Pensacola Gazette* and copied in the *Florida Mirror* on March 25, 1882: "Under the tutelage of that long-headed and far-sighted old gentleman, Mr. Yulee, [they] are awakening to the realization of the brilliant prospect that is ahead of them and their city."

To allow shipping to continue while construction of the south jetty was going on, engineers maintained a "sailors' gap" in the long line of jetty rocks. This allowed vessels to navigate through the opening of the gap and use the south channel. A movable front-range light to navigate the sailing gap was located on the sand dunes and mounted on a track with the lighthouse as the permanent back range. As the outer channel changed, the movable front

AIMH

The movable front range light.

range light could be adjusted on the track to show the deep channel. A rare navigation chart shows the sailing gap in the south jetty of the St. Marys Entrance.

Until completion of the jetties in 1903, periodic reports were made in the *Mirror* on the progress of work on the bar. By March 1902, 302,000 tons of rock had been deposited. The north jetty extended from the south end of Cumberland Island for a distance of three nautical miles; the south jetty on the north end of Amelia Island extended two nautical miles.

Update

The *Nassau County Leader*, on July 22, 1927, reported that rocks were being placed on the jetties to raise them six feet above low water: "The last barge of rock has been set in place ending the first improvement to the jetties since their construction."

A June 9, 1987, article in the *Florida Times Union* of Jacksonville describes an extensive and expensive reconstruction of the jetties in progress as part of a "channel deepening project to prepare King's Bay Naval Submarine Base for the mammoth Trident nuclear submarines." The crumbling south jetty was reinforced by "1,500 feet of interlocking concrete blocks."

According to Florida's Sea Grant Program *Glossary of Inlets Report # 11:* The north jetty, at present, is 19,150 feet, with a crest width of 8 feet at shore, and 15 feet at seaward end, 7 feet above mean low water. The south jetty, at present, is 11,200 feet, with a crest width of 8 feet throughout; 6 feet above mean low water."

Piers extending out over harbor waters allow rail cars to bring their loads of lumber and naval stores within feet of waiting ships in this 1902 image. Some remnants of these docks and pilings can still be seen today.

AIMH

Making a Living
Lumber and Naval Stores

The naval stores industry is one of the oldest American industries. As early as 1785, sources report that fifty thousand barrels of tar, rosin, pitch, and turpentine were gathered around the St. Johns and St. Marys Rivers. Without doubt some of this product was shipped from Amelia Island's harbor. The term "naval stores" stems from the pitch from resinous trees that has been used for thousands of years to keep the seams of wooden boats and ships from leaking. Noah's ark was sealed "within and without with pitch" (Genesis 6:14). Baby Moses floated in the bulrushes in a wicker basket "covered over with tar and pitch" (Exodus 2:3). Fleets of British, then American, ships depended on pitch to keep afloat. Besides tar and pitch and other refined products of resinous trees, the term naval stores gradually came to include lumber and other products used in the construction and maintenance of wooden boats.

Shortly before the end of the Civil War, William C. Morrill erected a "turpentine manufactory" about two miles from the town of Fernandina. A visitor from the North described this installation in a "Letter from Fernandina, Florida," published on March 1, 1865, in the *Boston Semi-weekly Advertiser*.

> Two of the vats are already finished. Sixteen condensers from the manufactory of Hixon, Badger, & Co. of Boston will soon be in operation and will make about 150 gallons of turpentine and 25 barrels

of tar per diem. About 60 men will be employed. 500 cords of pinewood have already been cut. A cord of wood will yield about 3 barrels of tar and 15 gallons of turpentine. The factory is located near the shore of the Amelia River and the transportation is done in lighters....Dwellings for the workmen will be built and a village will soon spring up.

It is not known if William C. Morrill's naval stores installation ever operated in the upheavals that followed the Civil War, but as the Florida Railroad was completed and shipping in the port of Fernandina boomed, the timber and naval stores of Nassau County and the surrounding area were in increasing demand. By the Golden Age, the shipping of lumber, turpentine, and rosin had become the major activity on Fernandina's riverfront. The docks were

It appears that this ship has loaded most of its naval stores that will soon be on its way to the north.

AIMH

piled high with cross ties, lumber, and naval stores products awaiting shipment to ports around the world.

One of the most important industries on Amelia Island after the Civil War was the Amelia Stem Sawmill owned by Colonel J. C. Read. Established in 1866, the mill was located on the Amelia River north of Old Town. *Webb's Historical, Industrial and Biographical Florida,* published in 1885, described the mill operation: "Thirty-five men work 10 hours a day at the mill to produce 30,000 feet of lumber, a yearly aggregate of 9,000,000 feet." The mill, *Webb's* reported, had never been without an order. In addition to the lumber sawed and sold from the Read's mill docks, an artesian well 250 feet deep was capable of furnishing 40,000 gallons of water per day to vessels loading lumber: "This water, slightly impregnated with sulfur, is famous for its purity and length of time it can be kept, and it is accordingly in great demand for seagoing vessels." J. C. Read used some of the quantities of sawdust and lumber from his mill to repair the boardwalk that extended to Old Town from North Third Street Fernandina (*Florida Mirror,* Sept. 16, 1882).

Read's mill and vessels loading lumber on the Amelia River just north of Old Town. It remained for decades as a major industry.

AIMH

Webb's also mentioned other lumber merchants: "Messrs. Wheelwright & Co., L. Bucki & Son, Geo. F. Drew, W. B. C. Duryee, G. W. Hipple & Co., Eppinger & Russell, and C. A. Fairchild have extensive docks along the harbor front. Messrs. L. A. Davis & Bro., Hilliard & Bailey, and J. Mizell & Bro. have large lumber mills upon the Saint Marys River and ship at this port. The lumber business.... will still further develop with the enlargement of railway connections in the interior with the lines of railway now terminating here."

The *Metropolis* of Jacksonville reported on March 29, 1900, that approximately nine million feet of lumber per month left Fernandina's port. The *Metropolis* also cited the thriving business in palmetto fiber, used to strengthen plaster, produced at a new factory built by Chas. R. Weeks & Bros. Palmetto fibers, the paper noted, were used in construction of Madison Square Garden and the Tampa Bay Hotel and "in many other triumphs of architecture too numerous to mention."

St. Marys River timber dealers such as the Davis and Mizell families floated enormous rafts of logs down river roped together through iron rings ("dogs") driven into the wood, and shipped finished lumber from their sawmills in the river towns of Crandall, Orange Bluff, or Kings Ferry to Fernandina docks for distribution to Europe, the Caribbean, and South America. Riverboats and tugs such as the *Dandy* and *Gladiator* were frequent visitors, bringing supplies to the families on the river and returning to Fernandina with cargoes of lumber and naval stores from Nassau County and southeast Georgia. Charles J. Davis, Jr., in the privately published *I Remember Crandall*, notes that as many as five sailing vessels could be seen loading at the Crandall docks, as well as the tugboats that pulled rafts of 1 to 3 ½ thousand board feet of logs down the river. Davis records that Crandall lumber sold for $27 per 1000 board feet and logs were $7 per 1000 in 1905.

As the timber and sawmill businesses began to run out of raw materials, the labor-intensive naval stores industries continued to provide jobs for hundreds of north Florida citizens. The gum of the pine trees, the source of naval stores products, was obtained by cutting slashes of intersecting chevrons on the face of a pine tree. In the early days, the seeping gum from the slash was collected in a "box" chopped with a "box ax" into the base of the tree. Later, metal gutters directed the flow of gum into clay pots or tin cups. Slashes may have extended ten or more feet up the side of the pine. In the infamous chain-gang era of Florida state prisons, prisoners could be hired to service the thousands of acres of pines on turpentine plantations. This practice, although legal and encouraged as revenue by the state, was filled with abuses

Kings Ferry and Orange Bluff began milling operations before the Civil War with the Germonds, Davis, Mizell and Hilliard and Bailey mills supplying ships with cargo shipped around the world.

JHJ

and exploitation, and was shunned by many landholders.

After collection, the raw gum from the pine tree was boiled in enormous vats, distilled into turpentine, and processed into rosin. The rosin was poured into barrels and graded according to the purity and color of the rosin. The purist and palest rosin was labeled WW for water white, WG for window glass, and X for the purest. The lowest quality rosin with the most impurities was labeled B for Betsy.

The contribution of the naval stores and lumber industries to Amelia Island's economy is evident in the shipping records found on the pages of the *Florida Mirror* and in photographs showing hundreds, even thousands, of barrels of turpentine and rosin on the docks at Fernandina. The *Mirror* published regular shipping records: "Spanish bark *Valvadore* loaded with 601,253 feet of lumber bound for Malaga, Spain" and "the *Lillian Roth* will take a cargo of rosin and cotton meal." Five other steamships sailed at the same time with approximately "20,000 of phosphate, 10,000 pounds of cotton meal, and several thousand tons of rosin, cedar logs, etc." "The schooner *Lizzie E. Dennison* cleared yesterday for Martinique, W. I., for Mizell and Bro. with a cargo of 368,000 feet of lumber." In the first quarter of 1882, Deputy Collector of Customs C. V. Hillyer reported in the *Mirror* that 5,338,000 board feet of lumber had been shipped, including "1,000,753 board feet for foreign ports," and "4,000 barrels of rosin waited to load for Liverpool."

Update

The timber and naval stores businesses had declined by the 1920s. As the depression deepened in the 1930s, landowners such as E. P. Davis, father of the author, Suzanne Hardee, sold their large tracts of pine forest to Rayonier or

Container Corporation to supply the inexhaustible needs of the newly-built pulp and paper mills in Fernandina. After lumber and naval stores, pulp wood was the third generation of prosperity to come from the area's forests. The last producers harvesting gum on Amelia Island were Leighton Shave and Frank Powell. They leased pine-land from the Afro-American Life Insurance Company, Dr. D. G. Humphreys, L. G. Hirth, and Nassau Truck and Farm Company. Shave and Powell terminated their turpentine operations in 1947. Today, a few pine trees with healed over "cat faces," the chevron shaped scars left when gum-yielding streaks were cut into the trunk of the tree, may still be seen on the south end of the island in one or two residential areas and along the fairways of golf courses.

The St. Marys river steamer Hildegarde departs the dock at Crandall on its way to Kings Ferry. Ladies watch as perhaps family members are on their way to visit friends at the old homestead.

Ernest P. Davis Family Collection

Making a Living
Agriculture

From the time of the Indians, fruits, vegetables, grapes, and other crops have been cultivated on Amelia Island. The town of "New Fernandina," in fact, was the site of an indigo plantation established by the Countess of Egmont. The local newspapers of the Golden Age often commented on the island's exceptional fruits and vegetables and their cultivation by local growers. The following examples show the incredible variety and productivity of farms surrounding Fernandina.

A letter to the editor, signed by "Looker On," appeared in the *Florida Mirror* on December 7, 1878. The writer of the letter described the Amelia Avenue property of W. F. Scott, the man for whom Scott Road near Amelia City is named. The Scott property was described as "arched by majestic, wide-spreading oaks, hickories and bays, draped with beautiful gray moss, making it indeed a charming spot where only two year since was a dense hammock, the retreat of wild beasts." The writer went on to say: "I found friend Scott busily engaged in erecting a sugar mill preparatory to grinding sugar cane.... I continued my trip down to Dr. Harrison's orange grove and found the Doctor manufacturing syrup."

The huge Harrison plantation syrup kettle, now on the grounds of Fort Clinch, is evidence of the quantity of syrup produced from Dr. Harrison's sugarcane crop. In the 1930s, Alice Youngblood, researcher for *Seeing Fernandina,* interviewed Morris Drummond, whose family had worked for generations of the Harrison family. Drummond described the immensity of the Harrison plantation syrup kettle and the quantities of syrup produced: "Missus, you could start boiling in January and next June, you'd still have juice to boil up."

Although little now remains of such prosperous agricultural ventures flourishing on Amelia Island and the surrounding area, an incredible variety of crops cultivated on the island were mentioned in Golden Age newspapers:

"Mr. George S. Roux has in his yard an olive tree from which he gathered two bushels of olives." "The *Mirror* is indebted to Mrs. George Roux for a jar of pickled olives" (*Florida Mirror,* Sept. 27, 1879, and Oct. 4, 1879).

Mr. M. Day, Jr. "was in town to demonstrate improved machinery for threshed, hulled and polished rice" (*Florida Mirror,* Mar. 1, 1879). "R. M. Witt placed on exhibition at the *Florida Mirror* the finest specimen of rice on the stalk we have seen" (*Florida Mirror,* Nov. 29, 1879).

"Mr. Isadore O'Neill has one of the finest farms in the state. He cleared the snug sum of $600 on celery" (*Florida Mirror,* May 21, 1881*).* The O'Neill farm was located across the Amelia River on the mainland. "Mr. W. F. Scott brought in a California winter white radish that was 12 inches long and weighed 2 pounds" (*Fernandina Express,* Feb. 11, 1882). Mr. Thomas Kydd, a downtown merchant, "produced 500 crates of tomatoes last season." Kydd also owned orange and peach trees, grape vines, LeConte pears, and bananas (*Florida Mirror,* Oct. 10, 1885).

"The prospects for the peach crop are bright" (*Fernandina Express,* May 21, 1881). "Mr. Warren Scott of Amelia this week presented the *Mirror* office a huge watermelon weighing 51 pounds" (*Florida Mirror,* July 12, 1884). "Mr. Kydd gathered 900 quarts of strawberries from somewhat over 1/2 acres"

(*Fernandina Express,* May 21, 1881). "Orange packing has commenced, but not yet full blast. At Dr. Harrison's place are the oldest oranges trees on the island. Harrison produced 150 gallons of syrup this year" (*Fernandina Express,* Nov. 20, 1880). "Among a lot of oranges sent by Dr. Harrison to Messrs. Angel and Friend, it was no difficult matter to pick out one weighing 18 ounces. They are not only large but deliciously sweet" (*Fernandina Express,* May 21, 1881). Matilda Seton McConnell, daughter of the first mayor of Old Town, in reminiscences written in 1880, recalled a fig tree in Old Town: "It is 60 years old, 40 feet high, its trunk, 56 inches in circumference, and yields abundantly."

"Mr. Cone brought into the *Florida Mirror* office palmetto leaves on which were hundreds of silk cocoons about the size of a large pecan and all shades of color. The cocoons are fed on Chinese mulberry and shipped to New Orleans" (*Fernandina Express,* Feb. 11, 1882).

"An egg, weighing 1/4 pound, and measuring 6x7 inches in circumference" was the extraordinary "fruit of Mr. P. I. Courter's hennery" (*Florida Mirror,* May 9, 1885).

The bounteous crops of onions, potatoes, squash, melons, beans, peas, cauliflower, sugar cane, rice, lettuce, oranges, strawberries, peaches, pears, grapes, and bananas grown on Amelia Island, plus those shipped into Fernandina by train from Central Florida, called for a "Market House," an ice house where these valuable crops could be safely refrigerated to await their use by local housewives, hotels, and boarding houses, or to be stored before their shipment to the North. The Market House, "built on the Centre Street Wharf," in 1883 was described as an "immense refrigerator." It was "so arranged with large ice chambers and non-conducting wall [so] that meat, poultry etc. can be kept in perfect order during the warmest weather" (*Florida Mirror*, Mar. 3, 1883). Ice for this purpose was shipped from Maine to Fernandina's ice-merchant W. K. Bauknight. Later, an ice manufacturing plant to supply the ice used for transporting fruit, vegetables, and seafood opened for business on May 12, 1891. The plant, located at 111 South Eleventh Street, was purchased in March 1896, by John W. Simmons (Jacksonville *Metropolis*, Mar. 29, 1900).

In 1880, Santiago Carrio, a native of Cuba, began to manufacture El Destino cigars at his establishment on Centre Street. In 1888, *Webb's* noted that "Mr. Carrio enjoys a lucrative trade, and his store is very popular." The *Jacksonville Metropolis* on March 29, 1900, observed, "Florida tobacco has a flavor peculiar to itself, and is in high standing with consumers of the [weed], equaling in flavor the finest grades of Havana. Mr. Carrio does a good business…." On May 18, 1898, the *Mirror* indicated that the "finest flavored Havana cigar tobacco" was still being locally produced.

The island area also boasted a fledgling but short-lived wine industry. An account in the *Florida Mirror* on December 21, 1878, of the State Fair held in Gainesville, mentioned that John Owens exhibited "native wine." The "St. Marys River Section" of the *Florida Mirror*, December 22, 1883, noted: "We are also glad to hear very encouraging news from the vineyard; thus Mr. Owens' vineyard (only a few years in bearing) had this year produced 900 gallons of good wine, in value $1800, and this product of only three acres." An Owens descendent recalls that the wine-producing vines were cut down when the lady of the family "got religion."

A poignant story that has persisted in the annals of Amelia Island agriculture appeared in the *Nassau County Leader,* on September 24, 1930. The article was about a Frenchman who came to Amelia Island in 1878, settling in the Amelia City area between the hammock and the beach. He developed a fine vineyard by grafting native grapes. When the Frenchman died, he asked to be buried on the highest sand dune facing his native France. For many years, a rough wooden cross marked his grave

Update

Perhaps the most lasting contribution of Amelia Island's agricultural history may be found in the camellias and azaleas bred by horticulturist Gus Gerbing in the Amelia City gardens he established in 1923 and operated until his retirement in 1948. The white *Mrs. G. G. Gerbing* azalea still graces gardens throughout the South.

A wagon carrying a load of passengers on their way to a cane grind.

AIMH

Amelia Island's pogy plant was on the north entrance of Egan's Creek where its remnants remain today. Here, originally, was the site of Read's Mill and later Nassau Fertilizer Company.

AIMH

Making a Living
Menhaden

The menhaden industry of Amelia Island is most likely recalled by older residents with fond nostalgia. It is as if the memory itself fills the air with the distinct, unforgettable odor of a pogy plant in operation—the odor that meant groceries on the table, the rent paid, and a new pair of shoes for many an island citizen. From the early 1870s, this industry held a prominent place in the island's economy along with that of phosphate, lumber, naval stores, and shrimping. Much of the following information on the menhaden companies operating out of Fernandina is taken from author John Frye's book, *The Men All Singing*.

The menhaden industry is one of the oldest in America. For generations, school children have been taught that Indians instructed the Pilgrims to fertilize their cornrows with menhaden fish, so it is not surprising that the name "menhaden" appears to have evolved from an Indian word meaning fertilizer. Fishermen and farmers soon observed that when the menhaden fish was mashed or stepped on, oil squirted out. This oily and abundant fish, first caught from rowboats in simple nets, cooked in kitchen pots, and ground with primitive grinders and presses, became the source of a valuable industry.

John Frye determined that the menhaden industry began in the state of Florida in the 1870s, centered in the towns of Mayport, Fernandina, Port St. Joe, and Apalachicola. Several menhaden plants have operated on Amelia Island—all in Old Town Fernandina. Among them were Mayport Fisheries,

Quinn Menhaden, the Fish Meal Company, owned by the Otis and Harvey and Gilbert Smith family, and Nassau Fertilizer and Oil.

Menhaden, locally called "pogy," is a member of the herring family. In other regions where the fish is harvested, it may be called "bunker," "mossbunker," "fatback," or simply "herring." Pogy fish swim in enormous schools—millions of fish swimming closely packed together like a dark underwater thundercloud. A day's catch processed at one of Fernandina's plants may have consisted of over 500 tons of fish. The schools of pogies were once spotted from a "crow's nest" high on the mast of the pogy boat. When the spotter discovered a school, the seine setter lowered a boat and quickly rowed toward the thick mass of fish. Using his oar, he signaled the location and movement of the school to the waiting purse boats; for instance, a spinning oar meant "Fish moving around. Don't come close!" Purse boats were motorized during the 1930s, and in later years, small planes located the huge schools from the air and radioed instructions to the boats for making a "set."

To make a set, the fish had to be surrounded by a purse seine which was drawn around the mass of fish by two purse boats, each loaded with one half of the seine, and each manned by a crew of eight or more strong men. The net, or seine, could weigh 8,000 pounds and was kept afloat by approximately 2,500 five-inch corks. The net surrounding the fish measured a quarter of mile long and sixty feet deep, rigged at the bottom with hundreds of galvanized metal rings, each weighing a pound. Purse lines threaded through the rings, and when pulled, closed the bottom of the net to make the "purse." As soon as the school of fish was encircled, the fishermen pursed the net to keep the fish from escaping through the bottom. To close the net, a five hundred pound purse weight, called a "tom," was dropped overboard. The weight of the tom pulled the lines through the rings and closed the bottom of the net into a bag. According to pogy boat lore, the term "tom" originated before the use of hydraulic motors and hoists, since on one boat a man named Tom was the strongest man of the crew and capable of lifting the heavy purse weight by himself. The pogy boat then maneuvered alongside the purse boats and a large suction tube lowered into the net to pull the fish into the hold.

In the days before power blocks and pumps to suction the fish into the boat, the real work of the day began when a successful set was made and the fisherman took on the task of raising the net loaded with tons of fish. "Bunt pulling," or raising the net, was hard labor. As many as twenty-six men would reach down from their purse boats and grab the meshes of the enormous net and pull it into the boat. At first, the net came up easily. Yard by yard, strong arms grabbed and pulled, forcing the thousands of fish to press together, or "harden," in the net. With each heave, the multitude of fish in the net were packed tighter and tighter and became heavier and heavier. Muscles as hard as iron began to strain and struggle. Then, a cry might be heard: "Put a nickel in the piccolo!" This was the signal for a colorful chantey unique to the menhaden industry that provided the rhythm or cadence for the raising of the heavy net. As soon as the men in the purse boats had hardened the catch as much as possible, the pogy boat moved in to load the catch into the hold. Loading the fish into the hold of the pogy boat was, again, backbreaking labor. The day was not done, however, until the fish were safely unloaded at the processing plant. In early years, the fish were bailed by hand with large dip nets, and later, by a large suction tube. With the advent of power blocks, winches, and pumps, the number of men needed for the long day's work was reduced from twenty-six, to ten or twelve, and later, to six or eight.

In the processing plant, the fish were cooked and pressed to remove the valuable oil and the remaining water and liquid. The dried and ground solids produced fertilizers and meal for livestock and poultry feed. The oils extracted from the menhaden were used in cosmetics, soap, paints, and lubricants.

Older residents of Amelia Island may recall standing on the beach watching a menhaden boat close in shore making a "set" and hearing the sound of a chantey wafted across a calm summer sea as the men in purse boats pulled the loaded net. Those watching on the shore may have heard a chantyman's salt-water-enriched voice strike up a song such as this:

> Wine, wine, wine.
> Oh my Lord
> Ought to be to Heaven ten thousand years
> Drinking of the wine.
> I got a mother in the Promised Land,
> Bye and bye I'll shake her hand.
> Ought to be to Heaven ten thousand years
> Drinking of the wine.
> Up on the mountain when Jehovah spoke
> Out of his mouth came fire and smoke
> Ought to be to Heaven ten thousand years
> Drinking of the wine.

Menhaden chanteys such as this were so well known that they were included in the concerts celebrating the one hundredth anniversary of Carnegie Hall.

Update

During the 1930s, a combined fleet of fifteen or more vessels left the processing plants on Amelia Island before daybreak during the months of May to November and returned each evening loaded with tons of fish. On June 10, 1927, the *Nassau County Leader* reported that Nassau Fertilizer and Oil was the "largest industry operating in Nassau County. Approximately 150 men are employed on the boats and the plant for eight to nine months of the year." Boats owned by the company included "the *Wallace M. Quinn,* the *MacIntosh,* the *Boys,* the *Seminole,* the *Carolina Vineyards,* and the *Grampus."* The *Leader* also reported that the Fernandina branch of the "Wallace Tiernon Company of Newark, New Jersey" was busy installing "a deodorizing plant," seemingly with mixed results in the perception of many Fernandina residents.

In the 1940s, a major part of the oil produced by Nassau Fertilizer and Oil was shipped to Europe for use in oleo and cooking oils. During World War II, the Stokeley Company canned menhaden fish packed in tomato sauce in the Fernandina plant. The cans' labels read "Silver Herring."

The Quinn Menhaden Company was established in Fernandina in 1931 when, at auction, the Quinns bought a local menhaden factory that had been seized by the government for "whisky running." The Quinn Menhaden boats were the *Wallace M. Quinn* and the *Benson Riggin.* In 1971, Nassau Fertilizer and Oil purchased the Quinn plant.

The Fish Meal Company was owned by W. B. Blades, A. R. Marks, J. T. Abernethy, and John Haverstick. The Fish Meal Company boats were the *Perkins,* the *Mace,* the *Blades,* the *Marks,* the *Storm King,* and the *Deutchland.* In 1930, according to John Frye in *The Men All Singing,* the Smith family extended their wide-spread menhaden business into Fernandina when they purchased the Fish Meal Company. By the 1950s, Otis, Harvey and Gilbert Smith owned a fleet of fifty menhaden boats on the Atlantic and Gulf Coast. In 1954, Mayport Fisheries, one of the Wallace Fisheries companies, rented the Smith family plant and operated out of Fernandina for four years. J. Clarence Taylor was supervisor.

The parent company of Nassau Fertilizer and Oil Company was the Seminole Oil and Fertilizer Company, one of the first companies in the state of Florida to harvest the once abundant menhaden. It later became Nassau Fertilizer and Oil, Inc. James B. Guess, Jr., was founder of the company. In 1978, James B. Guess III held the office of president and Exteen Corbett and his son James S. Corbett served as manager, secretary-treasurer, and assistant manager.

In 1960, Nassau Fertilizer operated three vessels: the *Lorikeet,* skippered by Captain Telford Gaskins; the *Barbet,* by Captain Otis Jones; and the *Tracy Corbett,* by Captain Lou Lokey. The *Lorikeet* and the *Barbet* were converted minesweepers from World War II (*Florida Times-Union,* Jun. 12, 1960). During the last years of production, Nassau Fertilizer operated two refrigerated boats and a Cessna Skyhawk spotter plane piloted by Herman Bowen. The boats were the *Novelty,* a 130 foot vessel with a capacity to hold 800,000 fish, and the *Jim Guess,* which measured 112 feet with an almost equal capacity as the *Novelty.* The *Novelty* was captained by Frank Lokey, who, when he retired, had spent fifty years in the commercial fishing industry. The *Jim Guess* was captained by James Williams and later by Otis Jones. These vessels each burned six hundred gallons of fuel a day.

Of the menhaden companies operating out of Fernandina, only Nassau Fertilizer and Oil remains in business today. In 1988, Nassau Fertilizer sold its last boat, due to a changing industry caused, in part, by foreign competition. Nassau Fertilizer and Oil has converted to warehousing, dockage, and some blending of feeds. With the sale of their last remaining boat the *Jim Guess*, the once thriving menhaden industry on Amelia Island, in fact in all of Florida, was brought to a close.

Willie Mae Ashley, author and archivist of the black history of Amelia Island, takes the following personal reminiscence of the pogy fishing life from an interview with Captain Neil Frink, Sr., one of Fernandina's best remembered pogy captains:

Captain Frink was born February 14, 1900, in Southport, North Carolina. He began commercial fishing at age seventeen as a crewman, but climbed the fisherman's ladder to become Florida's first black licensed captain of a menhaden fishing vessel. His experiences at sea span decades as a crewman, pilot, and finally as Captain, U. S. Coast Guard, license #412149.

During the interview, Captain Frink spoke of his great joy in working as a team with his mate, pilot, engineer, cook, and crewmen. Jokes, storytelling, shared personal experiences, and singing songs made the hardest manual labor pleasurable. He recalled how he and his dedicated crewmen, mate Lee Laster, and engineer James Harris made an awesome fishing team, respected up and down the coast. When there was a big haul of fish, the task of pulling them in was hard, very hard. Oftentimes he would come down from the pilot house, or captain's quarters, and join his crew with encouraging words, "'That catch is worth $100 a man if we can get 'em in....We CAN do it." Then singing a jolly creative fishing song, a song with a spiritual flavor mixed with words of the fisherman's language, Captain Neil's resounding bass voice would energize the crew and make them join in. The blending voices and rhythm of work would make a seemingly impossible task possible. The men were motivated by the fact that they were paid on shares. The bigger the haul, the bigger the pay.

Captain Frink was in charge of many ships owned by the nationally known companies of Wallace M. Quinn and Nassau Fertilizer and Oil. Among the vessels he skippered were the *Commander,* the *Esther Tower,* the *M. M. Mark,* the *J. L. Morris,* the *Lewis Brother,* the *Mary Ellen,* the *Port Mamma,* the *Richmond,* and the *Novelty.* Captain Neil was instrumental in helping many local and area fishermen launch their fishing careers. A remarkable industrious and courageous man, Captain Frink's long and fruitful life has exemplified all the best characteristics of men of the sea.

Captain Frink died on September 22, 1994. At his funeral, the minister spoke of Captain Frink's generous nature: "If Neil had a dime, you had a nickel." During his lifetime, Captain Frink saw pogy fishing change from an operation which depended largely on the physical strength and tenacity of the men on the boats to an industry of powerful diesel-fed ships equipped with amazing electronics and heretofore undreamed of mechanical and hydraulic power.

The few people left in Fernandina who remember the days when pogy fishing was the island's major industry recall many inimitable characters among the owners, plant managers, the boat builders, the net makers, the cooks, captains, engineers and crew. These people contributed, each in his way, to that unique way of life of which they were a part.

The contribution of John S. Robas to the industry is especially noteworthy. Robas introduced the innovative Puretic Powerblock to Atlantic and Gulf fisheries and literally changed the industry. With the use of this block, much of the bone-wrenching, time-consuming manual labor of pogy fishing was eliminated. John Robas was one of Fernandina's most colorful waterfront characters during the 1940s and 1950s. During World War II, his love of the sea led him to volunteer for service in the Navy. Disappointed that the Navy would not accept a one-eyed man, and with fierce determination to serve his country, he turned to the United States Army and dodged bullets on the battlefields of Europe. Robas, with a master's degree from Cornell University, when the war was over came to Fernandina on the *Barbet*, a World War II minesweeper that he had converted to a commercial fishing trawler. Frustrated that year by an unusual lack of shrimp, he converted the *Barbet* to fish for pogy. Later, he sold the *Barbet* to Nassau Fertilizer and Oil. With the *Barbet* fishing for Nassau Fertilizer, John bought a seventy-two foot steel trawler, the *Pelican,* and outfitted her for a research vessel chartered to the Fish and Wildlife Service. Robas was fluent in Spanish and, when the shrimping industry expanded into Mexican, Central and South American waters, he was in constant demand as a marine surveyor with the task of assessing damage and insurance claims for both boat owners and insurance companies. In addition to all of his commercial fishing activities, John Robas was well known as a writer of stories and articles relating to the industry. His articles were published in fisheries magazines and papers around the world. John Robas was a man ahead of his time in the fishing industry. He died of a brain tumor at age forty-five. On the waterfront, in awe of John's knowledge and capabilities, bunt-pullers said to one another, "That man so smart his brain jes burned up."

The following names, and of course there are others, represent some of the colorful, esteemed stalwarts of Fernandina's pogy industry. They were the strikers, setters, bunt pullers, cooks, engineers, captains, managers and owners—members of an ancient, revered, but dying industry: Abernethy, Allen, Bowers, Carinhas, Corbett, Cook, Crawley, Davis, Frink, Gallager, Guess, Guthrie, Halter, Haynie, Haverstick, Holzendorph, Kegler, Litrico, Lokey, Lucas, Marks, McKee, Morris, Price, Quinn, Richo, Riggen, Robas, Santos, Skipper, Smith, Sterling, Styron, Taylor, Telford, Teston, Wade, Wallace, and Williams.

This glimpse of Amelia Island's menhaden industry is dedicated to my dear friends Exteen and Jim Corbett and to the memory of John S. Robas, Cornell graduate, fisherman, master-owner of the *Barbet* and the *Pelican*, inventor, renowned international writer, marine surveyor and friend.

Bunt pulling off of the Florida coast.

Unknown Source

Making a Living
Shrimping

O n any pleasant night," reported George Goode in the *Fisheries and Fishery Industries of the United States for the year 1880,* a man fishing Fernandina waters "can readily secure three or four bushels of shrimp…The catch is boiled and dried for shipment to the north….In 1879 quite a business was carried on. Some 300 bushels of dried shrimp in crates or baskets having been sent to market in New York, Philadelphia, Savannah, Atlanta, Macon, Georgia, and Charleston, South Carolina." The writer further described the method of catching shrimp in the waters around Amelia Island:

Cast nets from 10 to 15 feet in diameter are generally employed….The shrimp and prawns do not approach the shore as thickly in the daytime as at night, so that fishing is mostly carried on after dark. Two men go out in each boat, one to paddle and one to manage the net. Captain T. E. Fisher [shrimp producer and dealer from Fernandina] records one unusual catch of 7 bushels made by 2 men in 3 hours time.

Thus from fertile local waters was born a Golden Age fishery that has since grown into an important international industry.

An 1890 booklet intended to attract business to the area, entitled *Fernandina and Nassau County: Its Resources and Advantages,* noted: "The export of fish and prawns (shrimp) has been carried on successfully here for some years on a moderate scale. The shrimp procured here are very large and of fine quality." A shrimp measuring seven and one half inches caught off the local docks was considered newsworthy in the *Florida Mirror* of May 20, 1882. The *Florida Mirror,* on December 27, 1884, listed "24 cans of Shrimp...aboard Mallory steamship *San Antonio,* carried this week for New York from this port." At this time, fishermen preserved most shrimp for shipment to Northern markets by boiling them in brine and drying them in the sun on wooden racks. In the 1870s, these dried Fernandina shrimp fetched as much as $.50 per pound in New York. Captain Fisher, Fernandina's major shrimp dealer of the time, shipped 12,900 pounds of dried shrimp to northern markets before abandoning the business in 1880.

By the turn of the century, government fisheries statistics indicated that local fishermen produced thousands of pounds of shrimp a year using the most primitive methods of fishing—rowboats, cast nets, and haul seines. Fernandina native son and raconteur Jack McGiffin called the earliest boats "small, bald headed schooners with no power."

Nineteenth century shrimping required little investment and produced little profit, but the winds of Fernandina's destructive 1898 hurricane brought an unexpected boost to the island economy. Sollicito Salvatore, a Sicilian merchant seaman, arrived in Fernandina when his ship was driven into port by the storm. Salvatore, his Sicilian name later Americanized to Mike Salvador, decided to stay in Fernandina. The immigrant's ambition and fresh view of Fernandina's opportunities led him to realize the economic potential of the shrimp business, and he mortgaged his newly-purchased house to finance his new venture. The Nassau County courthouse still has the papers in its files, dated June 12, 1899, for Salvador's chattel mortgage for the purpose of purchasing supplies "for producing, processing, and shipping shrimp." Shortly afterwards, Salvador's friend Antonio Poli and brother-in-law Salvatore Versaggi joined him, and soon many more European fishermen followed these pioneers to participate in Amelia Island's fast-growing shrimping industry. A meld of Sicilian, Italian, Portuguese, Greek and other European nationalities brought a cosmopolitan flavor to Fernandina's waterfront. Some of their names are interwoven in the fabric of shrimping's earliest years: Gianino, Tringali, Bassetta, Litrico, Salvador, Serra, Scandaliato, Fazio, Carinhas, Gigis, Ferlisi, John Santos, Manuel Jesus, Moreira, Majoni, Sunderman, Olson, Hansen, Sousa, Jenson, and Johnson. There were many more.

Mike Salvador began his business with great energy, experimenting with new methods of shrimping and looking for innovative ways to process, transport, and market his catch. Salvador soon abandoned the most common method of cast net shrimping for the more productive use of haul seines, basically large versions of the recreational beach seines used today. His next innovation was to use a power boat to pull the seine, greatly increasing efficiency and allowing boats to venture into deeper waters. Bar pilot William Jones Davis and Joseph Gianino also pioneered in this area. Fernandina's shrimp production soared. In 1906, Salvador formed S. Salvador and Company and began exploring ways to store and transport shrimp under refrigeration. By 1912, shrimping was Fernandina's most significant industry.

The following year, an additional innovation once more transformed the shrimping business, the development of a funnel shaped trawl rigged with weighted boards that held the net wide as it dragged the sea bottom. These "otter trawls," as they were called, had long been used in European and New England fisheries. In 1913, Salvatore Tringali designed a net adapted from a Sicilian sardine trawl. Captain Billy Corkum, a New England fisherman who had been enticed to Amelia Island waters by a run of bluefish in 1912, adapted a similar net used for halibut fishing in Northeast waters. These otter trawl-type nets, adapted for shrimping by Tringali, Corkum, and other local shrimp fishermen, dramatically increased production (*Amelia Now*, Spring 1992). According to historian Derald Pacetti, Jr., "A single fisherman, towing the trawl behind a power boat, could catch more shrimp in less time than six men working the cumbersome haul seine." "By 1917," Pacetti continues, "annual production exceeded two million pounds worth over $200,000." Captain Dave Cook and Captain Emmett Freeman are given credit for improving the otter trawl-type shrimp net by adding corners and wings. Freeman and William Burbank, Sr., became the premier net makers of the area in the early years of the industry.

Among other early local names remembered in the shrimping industry, some predating the Sicilians and other Europeans mentioned above, are Clark, Christopher, Davis, Lucas, Traeye, Drummond, Simmons, Dover, Wilder, Lovell, Little, Kelly, Morse, Merrow, Tapper, Evatt, Bennett, Jones, Hirth, Gorenflo, Goffin, Hardee, Merror, Ludwig, Salhman, Smith, Brooks, Sorenson, Peterson, Brazell, Scott, Richo, Richards, Fishler, and Ferguson. Not to be forgotten are the nicknames among the shrimpers: Kerosene John, Cap'n Eat Em Up, Poppa Joe, Popeye, Cap'n Skip Jack, Albatross, Cape Canaveral Bill, Beans, Hungry Jack, Hog, Seven finger Brown, Blue Nose Charlie, Snookie, and Jitterbug Joe.

Fortunately, as these pioneers increased local shrimp catches, improvements in transportation made distribution more efficient as well. Jack McGiffin, in his book *It Ain't Like It Was in the Good Old Days....No, and It Never Was*, described a "big celebration" in Fernandina when the first boxcar-load of shrimp was sent to New York. Shrimp had been shipped for years in barrels and boxes in the baggage car of a train, but McGiffin called the boxcar quantity a "big business: The refrigerator car was loaded right at the passenger station at Centre Street. The car was decorated with crepe paper and signs. There were the usual speeches and even a band to send the first car off properly. It was the beginning of an era. Fernandina was the *shrimp capital of the world.*"

By 1916, Derald Pacetti notes, as many as fourteen refrigerated freight cars would leave in a single day. By 1917, Fernandina's docks were home to over one hundred shrimp boats. Associated businesses were established to build and supply the industry. In the early years of the shrimping industry, Fernandina African Americans were the boat builders of the island, including Wizzie Biddle, Bill Rivers, Oscar Danburg, and in more recent years, Manuel Drummond. The growing industry eventually led boat builders from Greece to set up their ancestral businesses on the shores of the Amelia River. Mike Tiliakos, his sons Nick and Johnny, and his son-in-law, Demetrios Nicholas (Jimmy) Deonas, who had come from Santorini, Greece, in 1941, built over two thousand shrimp boats over a period of fifty years.

The Tiliakos men used centuries-old boat building techniques and tools brought over from Greece. A visitor to their boat yard might see oak ribs boiling in a twenty-five foot pot. After eight hours, the boiling process softened the wood and allowed the ribs to be bent to the curve of the boat hull. For years, dozens of oak "knees," searched out in the Nassau County forests and harvested for shrimp boat keels, lay seasoning in the mud of the riverfront site of the Tiliakos Boat Yard. When fully seasoned, these naturally bent oak knees were as hard as iron. Boats built by Stathus Klonaris and Mike Tiliakos eventually plied the shrimping waters from North Carolina to the Gulf, and eventually to Central and South America. One of the most noted of the Tiliakos-built boats was the *Dixie Queen*. For years, the *Dixie Queen* was winner of races held in the river to celebrate Fernandina's Shrimp Festival.

Processing Fernandina shrimp also brought prosperity. In addition to S. Salvador and Company's efforts, some of the catch was canned in pre-World War I days in several small factories in Fernandina and Saint Marys owned by the Gorenflo, Smith, Hardee, Merror, Davenport, and Brooks families. W. M. Brooks continued to can shrimp in glass jars until the early 1940s. Local historian Captain George T. Davis recalled that there was a shrimp plant and canning factory at Walker's Landing, now part of Amelia Island Plantation, operated by Herbert Williams, of the pioneer Williams family.

One of the most important businesses that evolved with the shrimping industry was the Standard Hardware Company, a ship's chandlery founded in 1900 by John and Noble

The Versaggi shrimp fleet.

Hardee. Ira William Hardee, Sr., a younger brother to John and Noble, eventually became the owner of the business. Standard Hardware distributed the shrimp nets built by generations of the Burbank family, as well as everything else a shrimp boat might need, from rope to rain gear. The Burbank family netmakers were sought out for their creative adaptations of the patterns of shrimp nets to accommodate different sea floors, species of shrimp, horsepower of the boat engine, and personal specifications of each boat owner. Standard Hardware Company's distribution of Burbank nets played a key role in helping Fernandina's shrimping innovations spread throughout the Southeast.

Update

Larger catches elsewhere, the evolution of larger boats, sophisticated electronics and freezing and marketing techniques gradually moved the industry from its birthplace in Fernandina to the entire Southeastern Atlantic and Gulf coasts and into an international world of commercial fishing. H. F. Sahlman was a pioneer in shrimping Mexican, Central and South American waters. The Sahlman boats were among the first to harvest Royal Red shrimp found in 1955 in the Gulf Stream off Key West. Through the sons who succeeded him, Ira Hardee, Sr.'s growing company became the Standard Marine Supply Corporation, the largest commercial fishing supply house in the southeast before the company was disolved in 2008. Standard Marine headquarters in Tampa had a staff fluent in various languages to serve the shrimping industry all over the world. Suzanne Davis Hardee, author of this book, served as vice president of Standard Marine at its Fernandina office following the death of her husband Ira William Hardee, Jr., from 1970 until her retirement.

Second and third-generation descendants of pioneer net maker William Burbank, Sr., built their famous nets exclusively for the Stan Mar companies for many years. During the peak shrimping seasons, with a full crew, the Standard Marine net makers can produce ten new nets per day, and in addition, make repairs to as many as a dozen nets worn and damaged in fishing. The internationalization of the shrimp industry is illustrated by an interesting request filled by the Standard Marine Company. The order specified completely equipping three shrimp boats so that they were ready to fish the Persian Gulf. The boats, loaded with supplies for several years, were lifted to the decks of freighters and shipped out of Tampa to Kuwait. Sadly, over-fishing in American waters, coastal pollution, high fuel prices, and the expansion of shrimp farming have driven all but a few shrimp boats from Fernandina's docks. Expansion into international markets is essential for the industry's future.

Amelia Now

Mike Salvador

Making a Living
Phosphate

Phosphate ore, an important component of fertilizer, was discovered in Florida in 1881, but it was not until 1889 that a booming industry developed when high-grade quantities of the substance were found in Marion County. The heavy rock required the deepest of harbors to accommodate the extreme drafts of phosphate-loaded ships and Fernandina's deep natural harbor filled the bill. Brought in by rail from central Florida mines, phosphate was first shipped from Fernandina in 1890, when records show that 10,428 tons were shipped. By 1897, phosphate shipping had risen to 171,496 tons.

The phosphate industry gave impetus to the prosperity of the last decades of the Golden Age. Mrs. Kate Bailey, whose husband Effingham W. Bailey had supervised the first shipment of phosphate from the port in 1890, gave credit to the phosphate industry for affording a comfortable living "for the hundreds of Negro longshoremen and all those connected with the industry." Mrs. Bailey said, "It was a colorful sight to watch the longshoremen and hear their rhythmic songs as they passed back and forth over a narrow runway." Mrs. Bailey recalled that her husband and J. G. McGiffin were in partnership for twenty-five years. Her son, Oswald, was also active in the business, which later became the Bailey Davis Company (*Fernandina News-Leader*, July 29, 1949).

From 1900 to 1912, Fernandina was one of the largest hard-rock phosphate ports in the world. The *Florida*

Mirror on May 18, 1898, reported that "Fernandina ships more phosphate to foreign ports than all ports in Florida and Georgia combined....We have elevators and storage houses...and dispatch from the elevators or cars which run up to the vessel's side." This efficient method was a far cry from the way the first phosphate ships were tediously loaded by hand-pushed wheelbarrows.

The first phosphate elevator was located approximately a half mile north of Centre Street. When this elevator burned on August 19, 1907, it was rebuilt as a larger, more efficient structure. 91Later, the phosphate facilities were moved to a site just north of the present Rayonier pulp mill waterfront where, at this location, it was served by fourteen hundred feet of docks. This phosphate elevator operated into the 1940s.

Even before the turn of the century, the port of Fernandina began to lose its lead position in phosphate shipping to Tampa and Jacksonville, but extensive shipping of phosphate rock, however, continued. Local newspapers

The fire that destroyed the first phosphate elevator.

AIMH

of the late 1800s and early 1900s reported ships with exotic names loaded with phosphate bound from Fernandina to ports all over the world. Among them were the steamship *Montauk*, the *Minterne*, the *Elton*, the *Iris,* the full-rigged *Sierra Miranda*, the schooner *Lizzie M. Parson,* the British schooners *Hibernia* and *Frank Huckins*, the Austrian steamship *Ida*, and the schooners *Gracie D. Buchanan* and the *Levi S. Andrews*. The *Nassau County Leader,* on July 26, 1925, reported the British steamer *Ethelaric* had loaded 1,200 tons of phosphate handled by Bailey-Davis Company and "The steamer had quite a number of Brazilian monkeys aboard and the owners did a considerable business here selling them to Fernandina people."

Kate (Mrs. Effingham) Bailey, in a nostalgic essay in the *Fernandina News-Leader,* on July 29, 1949, related that a week before she had heard the "last, long farewell whistle of the last phosphate ship, as it said goodbye to Fernandina."

The second phosphate elevator was built along the Amelia River and lasted into the 1940s.

AIMH

Making a Modern City
Newspapers

The very first newspaper on Amelia Island, possibly the first in Florida, was printed on December 19, 1817, under the "piratical government of Louis Aury." Under a Mexican rebel flag, Aury appointed himself commander of military and naval operations on Amelia Island. No known copy of Aury's newspaper, entitled *El Telegrafo de las Floridas,* exists; however, a pamphlet produced by Aury's press, labeled "Fernandina, December 23, 1817" remains in a private collection.

The *Fernandina News Leader* claims the distinction of being the oldest existing weekly newspaper in the State of Florida; however, a long list of newspapers published in Fernandina under various names preceded the current weekly *News Leader* and makes it difficult to trace a clear line of ancestry.

"A Centennial of Publishing" appeared in the *Fernandina News-Leader*, April 24, 1958. It is the source of much of the following information. An article in the Jacksonville-based *Florida Times Union,* December 27, 1964, commemorating the centennial anniversary of the paper, is another helpful source. Copies of the oldest Fernandina newspapers are scarce, but, where possible, additional information relating to dates of publication, editors, publishers, and proprietors of the Fernandina newspapers has been taken from the masthead of actual copies. Howard H. Davis, Jr., at one time owner and editor of the *Fernandina News-Leader,* has been a generous and reliable source of information relating to that publication. The "Florida Newspaper Project" grant administered by the University of Florida Library now provides the most authoritative listing of Florida newspapers and their holdings housed in libraries and museums.

What follows are bits and pieces of information about Fernandina's newspapers from the sources named above, as well as the *Florida Mirror*, City Directories, *Webb's Florida,* and a chart compiled by H. J. Belcher indicating the approximate time most of Fernandina's newspapers were in existence.

Florida News: In 1858, Joseph E. Rogero, publisher of the *Florida News* in St. Augustine, moved to Fernandina, and keeping the name *Florida News,* established the first newspaper since Aury's day on Amelia Island. The first issue was dated February 10, 1858. The last known issue appeared in 1861.

East Floridian: William H. Babcock published the East Floridian in 1859. Its last known issue was in 1861.

Peninsular: W. C. Morrill and J. K., and Lyman D. Stickney published a Unionist Republican newspaper entitled the *Peninsular,* in Jacksonville, Florida. The *Peninsular* was inaugurated on April 4, 1863. According to the *Times Union*, the *Peninsular* was the ancestor newspaper of the Jacksonville paper. The article stated that J. K. Stickney moved from Jacksonville to Fernandina where he was a "grower of olives," and "began publishing a paper." Stickney's Fernandina newspaper was also named *Peninsular.* Its last known copy was published in 1864.

Fernandina Courier: The *Courier* was published by J. M. Doty and Company in 1866, possibly earlier. W. S. Shober served as editor and proprietor. The last issue known appeared in 1867.

Island City: C. H. Allen published the *Island City* between 1869 and 1871.

Fernandina Observer: The *Observer* appeared from 1870 to approximately 1876. John S. Adams edited the paper in 1870.

In 1873, the Observer listed Charles Berg as "foreman;" M. Hammond, publisher, and William Walkins Hicks and Charles H. Berg "proprietors." The Fernandina Press Association, later publisher of the *Florida Mirror,* purchased the *Observer* September 12, 1874. It listed Charles Berg as "managing agent" (*Fernandina Observer,* Dec. 19, 1874). On February 5, 1876, the editor of the *Observer* commented: "The future course of the *Observer* will continue straight-away...narrow and thorny...."

Florida Mirror: The *Mirror* endured from November 30, 1878 until 1901. The first issue of the *Mirror* noted H. P. Trimble, publisher; Thomas A. Hall, editor; and A. B. Campbell and George Burnside, proprietors. George Rainsford Fairbanks, also known as the author of the first history of Florida, soon replaced Thomas Hall and edited the *Mirror* from 1879 to 1889. In 1881, the *Mirror* moved from 218 Centre Street to the Duryee building at 101 Centre Street (*Florida Mirror,* Feb. 9, 1881). Charles H. Berg, at one time "proprietor" of the *Observer,* was listed as publisher in 1886. Mr. Moore and Mr. Manucy were noted as publishers in 1887. In 1901, the *Mirror* consolidated with the *Nassau County Star* and ceased publication under its venerable name.

Nassau County Star: Established October 1, 1897, the *Nassau County Star* in 1901 merged with the *Florida Mirror.*

Fernandina Express: The *Express* first appeared in 1878. Jno. A. Whitney was listed as editor. Publication ceased in 1882 due to "ill health of editor Whitney." S. W. Manucy acted as editor in 1881, and later served as publisher of the *Florida Mirror.*

Fernandina News: The *Fernandina News* appeared between 1880 and 1894.

Fernandina Record: The *Record,* established in 1888, merged with the *News* (not the *Fernandina News* above) in 1910 to become the *Fernandina News Record.*

Unknown: The City Directory of 1900 lists a black publishing company located on Ash and Fourth Street. It is likely that a newspaper was published by this company, but as yet, no copies have been located.

Fernandina News Record: The *Fernandina News* and the *Fernandina Record* merged in 1910 to become the *Fernandina News Record.* Its last known issue was published in 1920.

Of all the many newspapers formerly published in Fernandina, the *Florida Mirror* was held in undisputed pre-eminence. The *Mirror* was the product of the Fernandina Press Association, a corporation formed in 1874 by founders David L. Yulee and Samuel A. Swann for the purpose of "publishing a newspaper and the execution of printing of all kinds." Information regarding the corporation may be found in a scrapbook kept by Elizabeth Swann Carroll, daughter of Samuel Swann. "Articles of conduit" for the proposed publication of the *Mirror* attested that the newspaper would "abstain from partisan politics; advocate an upright judiciary, and a cheap and honestly administered State government; never publish anything embarrassing or repulsive to modest, virtuous, or religious people, nor be unjust to individuals." It is evident that George Rainsford Fairbanks, editor of the *Mirror* from 1879 to 1889, sought to uphold the high principled "articles of conduit" inaugurated by Yulee and Swann. Speaking at a meeting of the Florida Press Association in 1883, Fairbanks made the following statement:

> It has come to be said that no prudent father of a family can take home a daily city paper until he has carefully scrutinized its contents, there being so much published which is unfit for the eye of the young or of the gentle sex; and if unfit for them, why fit for

anyone? Let it be our aim to make our standard higher and better as a tradition to our successors and finally let us cultivate amenity and pleasant courtesy in all things (*Florida Mirror*, Feb. 17, 1883).

Fairbanks was a superb journalist. His editorials were savored not only by local readers but were often copied in other newspapers. Throughout Fairbanks's editorship, he continually touted what he believed to be Amelia Island's golden economic opportunities such as the deepening of Fernandina's harbor and what he proposed as a "great ship canal across Florida from the Saint Marys River through the Okefenokee Swamp, westward to Saint Marks along the Gulf coast" (*Florida Mirror*, Mar. 25, 1892). He was fearless in his editorial advocacy of his favored political candidates and in his endorsement of selected legislative measures. He was equally fearless in his opposition to the candidates he did not like and the legislature he did not espouse. Besides local and state news, Fairbanks filled his newspaper columns with current national and international news and essays on the histories of Florida, America and Europe. He reprinted stories of Uncle Remus, the writings of William and John Bartram, and provided his female subscribers with the latest fashion tips and trends.

Fortunately, many copies of the *Florida Mirror* still exist in museums, libraries, universities, and in the State Library in Tallahassee. In these copies, one may read a variety of editorial comment, some surprisingly current. For instance, a *Mirror* editorial, dated March 19, 1881, proposed that the Legislature of Florida should take action to prohibit the sale of "pistols, dirk and bowie knives." The *Mirror* later proposed the imposition of a substantial tax to slow the purchase of the deadly weapons, and thereby lessen "intemperances and crime" (*Florida Mirror*, Feb. 23, 1884). The *Mirror,* on July 26,

1884, urged, "Put a stop to carrying pistols." *Webb's Florida,* published in 1885, described the *Florida Mirror:*

[The *Mirror* is a] handsomely printed and well-edited newspaper published every Saturday at One Centre Street. It is an 8 page, 40-column sheet, devoted to home and state news enjoying a large subscription list and lucrative advertising patronage. The *Mirror* was established in 1878. Its increase has been rapid and in the period elapsed; its original size has been doubled. The composing and pressrooms are in the second story of the handsome brick structure known as the Duryee block. A Campbell press is used. For the jobbing department, a Gordon, and a Universal are used. Bookbinding and stereotyping are also done.

AIMH

A charming and trenchant summation of working for this small town newspaper appeared in the *Florida Mirror* on June 14, 1879, as proprietor A. B. Campbell said farewell as he "severed connection" with the *Mirror* for an unknown cause:

Life of a country editor is a strange mixture of joy and sorrow, fun and misery. He can learn more of human nature, its true inwardness or outward cussedness in 6 months than he otherwise could in as many years. He ought to be an angel or a devil, a lamb or a lion at will to suit the occasion. He must have a hide as thick as a rhinoceros and as soft as a kid. He must do 5 to 100 dollars worth of advertising for state, county and church fairs, concerts etc. and receive in return a complimentary ticket worth 50 cents, and if he brings his mother-in-law with him, he has to pay for her at the door. He gets more cussing and less blessing, does more for nothing, and gets less for much than any man living....He must smile when he is saddest and look sad when he is smiliest; and through all his troubles be thankful for the noble exception to the general rule. Yet withal there is something really fascinating in the profession, and I confess I leave the ranks with many regrets. In the language of Cataline to the Roman, 'I go but I may cum again.' Not *adieu* but *au revoir.* A. B. Campbell.

Update

Nassau County Leader: This paper was established on December 15, 1920, at Callahan by 20-year-old Crickett Prewitt. Prewitt moved to Fernandina and his newspaper absorbed the *Fernandina News Record* to become the *Nassau*

County Leader. The *Nassau County Leader* was later owned and edited until 1941 by Vesta Prewitt, daughter of the original owner.

The Outlook appeared for a short time in the 1930s.

The *Buccaneer,* edited by Harry Peace, was published from 1955 to 1959. Peace later moved to New Orleans where he published the *Fishing Gazette,* a noted commercial fisheries magazine.

The *Amelia Island Sun* lasted briefly from 1975-1976. Ron Sapp was editor; John Hill, publisher; Ronnie Head, advertising manager; and Renée Duncan, feature editor.

Florida-Georgia News: W. Chester King, Howard H. Davis, Jr., and Harry Peace established the *Florida Georgia News* in 1937 and Davis became editor. Previously, due to the fact that postal permits at that time were difficult to obtain, Chester King purchased the name and postal permit of a defunct Woodbine, Ga., newspaper. He also purchased a small Hilliard newspaper and its postal permit. This paper was named the *Hilliard Hen,* its masthead reading "It cackles now and then." King and Davis also owned and published the *Southeast Georgian,* a Kingsland area newspaper. Briefly, the *Florida Georgia News* was printed and mailed from Kingsland, Georgia. Howard H. Davis, Jr. bought out the Peace-owned *Buccaneer.* The name *Florida Georgia News* was changed to the *Fernandina News.*

Fernandina News-Leader: The *Fernandina News* became the *Fernandina News Leader* in 1946, updated to the *Fernandina Beach News-Leader* in October 1959. Since 1946, several owners and editors have published this weekly newspaper. In 1972, the *Fernandina Beach News-Leader* was purchased by the New York Times Company, and at present, is published by Community Newspapers, Inc., as the *News Leader.*

Making a Modern City
Schools

Oｎe may be certain that education was an important part of family life for the intelligent men and women who gathered to build a railroad and the new town of Fernandina. The following is not written as a comprehensive history of schools on Amelia Island, but merely relates a few highlights.

Unfortunately, very little is found pertaining to the earliest schools in Fernandina, although it is known that during the Civil War years, "women from the North" established two schools for freed blacks in Fernandina. The remarkable dedication of these women did much to prepare the long oppressed black people of the island for the responsibilities and challenges of their new social and economic condition. We may catch a glimpse of these Freedmen's Schools from an April 30, 1863, article in the *Peninsula,* a Unionist newspaper published in Fernandina.

Among the best of these schools, we rank those of Fernandina. There are now here over 300 scholars, divided between two schools. The primary school, where the children are taught until they can read, is held in the Presbyterian Church, and is under the immediate control of Misses Smith and Harris, two ladies from the state of New York. The school numbers over 20 pupils, of all ages from six years upward, but mostly young, and has a regular daily attendance of over 120, which is increasing continually as the black population of the island gains accessions from slavery. They are here taught words and letters and as soon as they can read simple sentences and form letters on their slates, they are transferred to the higher school. The exercises are varied so as not to become irksome. Every child learns to sing and they acquire a great variety of patriotic and religious songs so as to sing them with energy and harmony. They repeat the days of the week, months of the year, the names of the states, the President, etc., etc.

The other or higher school is held in the Episcopal Church, and is under the superintendence of Miss Merrick, a lady from Syracuse, N.Y. and Miss Foorz, a sister of Mrs. Col. Hawley, from Conn. It numbers 130, with a regular attendance of over 100 scholars. The attendance in both schools varies, owing to the lax and disorderly habits of parents and many inconveniences at their homes, but as a general thing the pupils are so interested that they are eager to come, and the severest punishment to them is that of being sent home for disorderly conduct. In this school the pupils are each supplied with slates and books, furnished by the friends at the north, and are taught from the black-board, and all practice forming letters and figures on their slates, to add and subtract simple numbers, etc. Here also the exercises are most judiciously varied so as to keep up the interest of the pupils through the entire session of three or four hours daily.

These lady teachers, who have left their northern homes on this labor of love, devote themselves to their self-denying patriotism and the most exalted Christian philanthropy…. It is really touching to see the simple evidences of affection of these children for their teachers in the daily offerings of beautiful flowers with which they literally load their tables.

The school rooms are tastefully and beautifully adorned under the direction of the teachers, with boughs of evergreens interspersed with pictures, the gifts of friends and mottos of 'Liberty a nation's glory.' 'We are free.' 'On earth peace, good will to men.' 'Freedom' (and) 'A Little child shall lead them.'

Chloe Merrick, director of the high school described above, was one of the "women from the North" who came south to teach and assist the newly freed slave communities. Born in Syracuse, N. Y, in 1832, she arrived in Fernandina in 1863 and became supervisor of the Freedmen's Relief Association schools. Harrison M. Reed, then Direct Tax Commissioner in the State of Florida, visited Fernandina in 1864. Impressed with Miss Merrick's work with the Freedman's School, he used his influence to help her purchase Confederate General Finegan's large three-story home to establish an orphanage in Fernandina for children of both races. The unmarried teachers of the Freedmen's Association lived there as well. Esther Hill Hawks, who kept a diary during the Civil War years, wrote of a visit to

Confederate Gen. Joseph Finegan's home became a Freedman's School and later the Bishop's School. AIMH

Chloe Merrick in Fernandina. In *A Woman Doctor's Civil War Diary,* Hawks described her visit to the orphanage:

"Great roomy house surrounded by verandahs and hemmed in with trees which enclose a beautiful yard. The house is comfortably furnished and has now 18 little orphan children residents...they all looked neatly dressed and contented... Four teachers live there, fine intelligent ladies. Ladies with hearts in their labors."

Although the institution that began with such promise closed in July1866, Chloe Merrick's selfless determination to bring education to neglected and underprivileged children won her the title of "Freedom's first lady." She also became the first lady of Florida when, on August 10, 1869, she married Harrison Reed, now Reconstruction governor of Florida, whose admiration of her during his visit to Fernandina seems to have been not merely respect for her professional accomplishments. The *Journal of the Florida House of Representatives* of 1871 recorded that the public school system had been established by the Florida Legislature six months after Chloe Merrick's marriage to Governor Reed, so she may have exerted gentle influence on the legislation.

The years following the Civil War brought increased financial support of public education from the state of Florida. State leaders were growing increasingly aware of the value of education for all. According to *Seeing Fernandina,* bids were let in 1875 for construction of four public schools on Amelia Island. C. W. Lewis, owner of the Tabby House on Seventh and Ash Street, became superintendent of schools the following year. Teacher salaries were set at $25 per month, and, if there were more than fifty scholars in the school, an assistant was hired at a salary of $20. *Seeing Fernandina* stated that the first public school was located on the corner of Sixth and Broome Streets. This school consisted of two large rooms and two playgrounds, one for the boys and one for the girls. *Seeing Fernandina* also recounts the anecdote that at one time the headmaster of the school was said to be tubercular. Believing that watercress was good for his illness, he would send the children down to the nearby wetlands to gather his medication.

On August 13, 1881, the *Fernandina Express* reported that the current county School Superintendent W. A. Mahoney "gives notice that the public school will be opened on the first Monday in September. The four-mill school tax will give the schools a four-month session." On October 1, 1881, the *Fernandina Express* reported that Mr. W. Thomas of Baltimore would be in charge of Public School Number One, coming highly recommended. Mr. Thomas cautioned, "It is important that parents and guardians insist in prompt and regular attendance of the pupils."

Unfortunately, Superintendent Mahoney gave a doleful report on the condition of county schools' progress only a few months later in the December 10, 1881, *Florida Mirror.* He reported forty-two Nassau County school districts. Most schools were in session for four months, but three schools still had three month terms. Reasons given by Mahoney for the short term were that the children had to work on the farms; parents were indifferent; and a few of the teachers had their certificates revoked.

A year later, Mahoney reported that five of the county schools had a noticeable lack of attendance due to the student's need to "assist on the farm," but happily school terms at the time had increased by then to six months (*Florida Mirror,* Apr. 5, 1882). Superintendent Mahoney published a "Public Notice" to teachers that they would be required to take examinations "in order to elevate the status of our public schools. The exam will be thorough" *(Florida Mirror,* Aug. 5, 1882).

L. W. Higginbotham became superintendent of schools after W. A. Mahoney. He announced in 1883 that "School #1 was opened last Monday with 60 scholars....The outlook for public schools in this city very encouraging" (*Florida Mirror*, Oct. 13, 1883). Higginbotham informed his teachers that they were required by order of the State Board of Education to use the following text books: *Robinson's Arithmetic, New Graded American Education Reader, Swinton's School Geography, Webster's Dictionary, Well's Shorter Course in Grammar, Swinton's Word Speller, Catherine Card's Literary Reader, Hart's English Grammar for Advanced Pupils* and the *Spencerian Copy Book* (*Florida Mirror*, Oct. 20, 1883). By October 11, 1884, the *Florida Mirror* quoted from Higginbotham's annual report that forty-four schools in Nassau County were now teaching 1425 students, including 661 black children. The annual budget for salaries for the school system was $5,745.43.

Mercedes Ray, in an article published in the *Fernandina News Leader* on February 2, 1994, stated that the first black public school on Amelia Island was a four-room two story building on North Eleventh Street. The *Florida Mirror* reported on this school on April 1, 1882, "The efficient head of colored public school now has 300 pupils, 4 teachers." In modern terminology, this school would have had a student/ teacher ratio of one teacher per seventy-five students! Ms. Ray noted that six teachers were later employed and Professor Moses Payne served as principal. Young William Henderson Peck, a graduate of Howard University, assisted Professor Payne. In 1880, Nassau County African Americans petitioned for a high school. A new school was accordingly constructed in 1884, although a full four year high school curriculum was not offered until 1908. In 1887, when Mr. Payne succumbed to yellow fever, the Superintendent appointed William Peck as principal of the high school. Serving as principal for fifty years, Peck was a very successful and beloved educator, and in 1928, the fine new school at 516 South Tenth Street was named for him. William Peck died in 1950, after a lifetime of service dedicated to the education of Fernandina's black children.

In 1896, a new school for white children was constructed at Centre and Ninth Streets. This school, now remembered as The Old School House, served until 1927 when students picked up their books and marched east down the street to occupy a more spacious facility that had been built on the site of six Indian mounds directly across from Central Park. This building accommodated all twelve grades until 1950 when Atlantic Elementary School was built on adjacent property to house grades one through six. High school students moved to a new facility on Citrona Drive a few years later.

Many notices of private schools are found in the local newspapers of the Golden Age. The *Fernandina Courier,* on January 2, 1867, advertised a boarding and day school for young ladies—Mrs. A. M. Bacon and Miss Florence O'Neill principals. "Higher English branches $22, Latin and French, $20, Music $35, and Drawing, $18." Board could be had on reasonable terms. The Reverend J. H. Myers of the First Presbyterian Church advertised a "Nassau College for young ladies with a thorough English education with special advantages in painting, drawing, music, and French" (*Florida Mirror,* Jan. 25, 1879). The *Fernandina Express* reported on May 21, 1881, that Mr. R. E. Alexander would open a "Private school in the Baptist Church on the 16th of May, and respectfully solicits a liberal share of patronage at moderate terms." In 1884, Mrs. L. G. Watson ran a select school for young girls on the northeast corner of Seventh and Centre. The girls were taught "decorative painting and embroidery" (*Florida Mirror,* Aug. 23, 1884). Miss Eunice Browne was principal of a school located between Calhoun and Broome on Second Street, called the "Fernandina Seminary for Young Girls." She taught the highest branches of English, French, music, and drawing. According to an advertisement in the *Mirror*, Miss Browne anticipated that a "building for chemical and philosophical apparatus would be secured as soon as the number of advanced classes will warrant the outlay" (*Florida Mirror*, Aug. 27, 1881). G. W. Schuyler was headmaster of a "Select Intermediate School for Boys and Girls located on the corner of Ash and Ninth Street." Pupils received instructions in vocal and instrumental music and French (*Florida Mirror*, Feb. 10, 1883). Also noted is the fact that Schuyler's pupils celebrated Washington's Birthday with a picnic at Fort Clinch.

The most prominent of the private schools on Amelia Island during the Golden Age undoubtedly was the "Episcopalian Academy of St. Mary's Priory," sometimes called the Bishop's School, located in the three story mansion built by General Finegan, the previous site of Chloe Merrick's orphanage. The Priory operated from 1869 to 1874. In 1871, two nuns of the Sisters of St. Joseph's order came to Fernandina from their mother house in St. Augustine to teach Fernandina's Catholic children. By 1884, they had built a fine convent and school. The school, located next to the Catholic Church, is still in operation today as St. Michael's School. For further information about these schools, see the Amelia Island Museum of History publication, *The Golden Age of Amelia Island—The Churches*.

An eternal verity regarding education was found in the *Mirror*, on January 22, 1881: "The perpetuity of good government and well-being and happiness of the human race depend very largely on the education of the masses of people...Let parents do their part toward our schools."

Making a Modern City
The Library

The men and women of the Golden Age of Amelia Island knew the importance of establishing libraries to complement the schools in their thriving community. Mr. C. H. Huot, a public spirited businessman of the Golden Age, established the first known library, a reading room at the rear of his new brick building at 12 North Second Street. This room was "kept especially for the use of captains of vessels…. [Its] large comfortable reading room is supplied with all the leading maritime and other newspapers" *(Florida Mirror*, Feb. 8, 1879). The Presbyterian Church bulletin on April 12, 1908, announced "A Service for Seamen in the Free Reading Room on North Second Street," so apparently, Huot's reading room was in use for at least three decades.

A public library for Fernandina's residents was founded shortly after Mr. Huot's seaman's library. An organizing meeting was called to take place at the office of Major W. B. C. Duryee *(Florida Mirror*, Feb. 7 1880). The attendees elected the Reverend Dr. J. H. Myers, minister of the Presbyterian Church, to be chairman of the committee to organize the "Library Association," assisted by five respected members of the community, "Mr. Whitney, Mr. W. H. LeCain, Samuel A. Swann, C. A. Choate, and Dr. Pope" *(Florida Mirror*, Feb. 11 1880). The committee proceeded to draft the articles of incorporation, and selected the following officers: President, the Reverend Dr. J. H. Myers; Vice-president, the Honorable H. J. Baker; Secretary, Mrs. John A. Whitney; Treasurer, Major W. B. C. Duryee; and Librarian, Mrs. John A. Whitney.

Directors included many familiar Fernandina names: Messers Samuel A. Swann, Thomas Kydd, W. H. LeCain, Norman Brownson, J. A. Edwards, E. P. Noyes, John MacKenzie, Fred W. Hoyt, and Charles A. Choate. Capital stock in the organization was set at $1000. As a fund raiser for the newly organized Association, "Fanny Wallack's Pinafore Burlesque Opera Company" and "Wallack Tripologue" performed successfully for two nights at the Lyceum *(Florida Mirror,* Feb. 21, 1880).

Whether a public library actually resulted from this Library Association is unknown, since the next mention of a library in the *Florida Mirror* occurred more than a decade later, when, on February 6, 1891, Major George Fairbanks called another organizational meeting to order. The following information is found in the original minute book of the Library Association:

In response to invitation of Mr. Samuel A. Swann, the citizens of Fernandina assembled on the upper floor of his new building at the corner of Center (sic) and Fourth Streets this Friday evening February 6th A.D. 1891. At the hour of eight o'clock the assemblage was called to order by Major George R. Fairbanks who briefly stated the object of the meeting and at whose request, Mr. Fred W. Hoyt read the text and terms of a formal lease under which Mr. Swann proposed to place certain apartments in his said building at the disposal of a duly constituted society for the purpose of a Library, Reading Room and Gymnasium. Mr. Robert S. Schuyler was then chosen temporary chairman, and Mr. Bernard T. Burchardi, temporary secretary.... The articles of the Association were read and a large number of persons constituted themselves members by signing the articles of Association....

Addresses made by Reverend J. B. Morton, and Major George R. Fairbanks gratefully acknowledged the public spirited benevolence of Mr. Swann who had designed and perfected the plan of a Reading Room, Library, and Gymnasium. A permanent organization was effected as follows: President, Henry E. Dotterer, Secretary, Charles Hillyer, Treasurer, R. Clifton Cooley, Executive Board, Mr. Samuel A. Swann, Mrs. Thomas Kydd, Mrs. W. B. C. Duryee, Mr. Fred W. Hoyt. All present inspected the gymnasium and facilities.

Subsequent minutes in the original minute book of the Association reveal that a $15.00 "honorary membership" in the organization included a family "except for sons over 15 years of age and children under 10 years." A $6 membership "shall include individual male subscribers over 16 years of age." $3.00 bought a junior membership, which "shall include lady and children subscribers (not members of family of honorary members.)" $25 was appropriated for a "lady librarian" who at her own expense "shall be responsible for a janitor." The good order and discipline, or lack thereof, of those using the library facilities would be "confided to Proctors selected from the board." The use of tobacco of any form was "positively prohibited in all rooms, under penalty of expulsion..... No lunch, fruit or other edibles shall be eaten in any of the rooms." On February 10, 1891, the Executive Board approved the following list of monthly periodicals: *Harper's Magazine, Scribner's, Century Magazine, St. Nicholas, Scientific American, Youths Companion, N. Y. Evening Post,* and the *Forum.* Newspapers included the *Times Union* and the *Standard* of Jacksonville, the *Boston Herald,* the *Philadelphia Daily,* the *St. Louis Republican,* and Fernandina's *News* and *Florida Mirror.* The *New York Herald, Puck,* and *Judge* were to be purchased from local dealers. After much deliberation, hours for the gymnasium, also located in the library's building, were finally determined: "Ladies—Monday, Wednesday, and Friday, until six o'clock." "Men and Boys—Tuesday, Thursday and Saturday, and also, every night in the week, from 6 to 10 p.m...."

At meetings following the organization, the board and officers offered free usage of the library and facilities to clergymen and their families and also to newspaper proprietors. A sign at the entrance door was installed: "LIBRARY and READING ROOM: STRANGERS WELCOME." The board accepted the gift of a complete set of Dickens and rejoiced that certain periodicals and newspapers were made available by the publishers to library patrons without charge.

As years passed, the minutes of the library meetings show a struggle to meet the expense of books, periodicals, lights, water, and insurance. As a source of income, the gymnasium was offered to the young men of the town for dances. The financial struggle continued until finally the librarian had to be dismissed and the ladies of the Association membership "took turns keeping the library open." Mrs. Thomas Kydd was a stalwart. In the "Woman's Edition" of the *Florida Mirror*, in September of 1900, she gave credit to the ladies of the Association for keeping the library in operation. Mrs. Kydd described the facility with considerable pride:

> The reading room is large and commodious, airy and cool in summer and in winter, always warm and comfortable. The shelves are well filled with carefully selected books in every line; history and biography, science, religion, poetry, fiction and books of travel, books for the young and books for the old. On the table are found the leading magazines of the day, and daily northern and state papers.

Update

The Library Association's original minutes end on March 13, 1896, and resume on February 23, 1923. On that date, the minutes record the Association's meeting for the first time in the Yulee Community House on North Third Street. The Community House was the former residence of city founder and United States Senator, David L. Yulee. Yulee's daughters had presented their family home to the city of Fernandina for a community house and for a "charming and permanent home for the Library." In the minutes of February 23, 1923, President Mrs. N. B. Borden instructed Secretary Emma Williams to write "a note of thanks to Mrs. Noble and Mrs. Neff [Yulee's daughters] for the many benefits received from them."

A few sparse Association minutes written in the 1920s and 1930s record Library activities such as a "Story Hour for children each Saturday morning at 10 A.M. led by Miss Emma Williams and Miss Nell Davis." An advertisement of the location, hours, etc. of the library was to be shown at the "Moving Picture Theater." The grim search for funds to buy books and pay a librarian's salary continued to hound the faithful board. A request for a contribution was made each year to the Carnegie family of Cumberland Island, and a gratuity of twenty-five dollars per month from the city helped to keep the doors open. The librarian's salary was later reduced to fifteen dollars a month, and hours were shortened. Beloved librarians of this period were Miss Frances Carrio and Mrs. Edith Chadwick Flood. The last entry in the Association's original minute book is dated September 29, 1935. An unsigned statement of condition of the Library Association written on a loose-leaf page is found inserted in the minute book. This page contains the following information: "136 books purchased," including a book on the subject of seashells, another on birds of Florida, and "a new edition of the *Britannica.*" The statement continues, "Approximately 4060 volumes in the Library, 129 subscribers, and 2755 books withdrawn."

Older citizens of Fernandina have fond memories of the Public Library located in the Community House, its brief return to its original quarters in the Swann building, and its move in 1943 to the 1886 school house at Eleventh and Centre Streets. The following unsigned notation appears in the original minute book: "The Library moved to the Community House in 1922, moved back to the Waas [Swann] Building in 1937, moved to Masonic Temple [Old School House] in 1943." In 1967, the Library moved from the Old School House to 210 Centre Street, and, in 1970, to its present location at 25 North Fourth Street. The Library Association, founded in the Golden Age, resulted in a library that continues to be a source of pride in the island community. It is the oldest civic organization on the island, and has continuously served the community for over a hundred years.

Making a Modern City
The Fire Department

O n March 23, 1876, a destructive fire swept through downtown Fernandina. Wooden buildings north of Centre Street were burned to rubble. Thomas Kydd's brick building at 301 Centre Street stood alone on what was once a bustling landscape. After the fire, the town quickly rebuilt, and once again, Fernandinians erected a thriving downtown, with stores and businesses once more made of wood. The *Florida Mirror* reported on July 26, 1879, that the Fernandina Hook and Ladder Company had petitioned the City Council to provide more and better fire apparatus. Not until September of that year did the city respond, albeit weakly, by ordering the reorganization of the languishing Fernandina Hook and Ladder Company (*Florida Mirror*, Sept. 6, 1879). Adequate financial backing from the city for appropriate equipment, however, was not forthcoming, so the Hook and Ladder Company urged the public to participate in securing "picks, axes, and ladders.... We are in danger at every moment of suffering from the Fire Fiend and powerless to subdue him" (*Florida Mirror*, Oct. 11, 1879). A subsequent letter to the editor of the *Florida Mirror* on June 2, 1882, once again warned city fathers, "We have no fire extinguishing apparatus and no water except that in the harbor to rely upon in case of an emergency." Still, the warning was not heeded.

In a city primarily constructed of wood and lacking adequate fire protection, another disaster was waiting to happen. In September 1883, another conflagration threatened Fernandina's downtown. A block of wooden buildings between Second and Third Streets, this time south of Centre Street, burned to the ground. The *Mirror* of

Two devastating fires leveled downtown Fernandina in the 1870-80s.

September 8, 1883, reported the following losses: "Streety's Tin Shop, F. C. Suhrer, Arthur Steil, Mrs. G. H. Latham, Mr. Beard, G. Stark, and B. W. Southwick....The Post Office on the west side of Second Street was saved by a bucket brigade."

The 1876 fire pictured below consumed the courthouse and all records.

Prominent citizen Robert Schuyler wrote a letter to the editor and advised succinctly, "The moral of the fire—get adequate fire apparatus."

A petition, submitted to the City Council and "signed by 22 young men," appeared in the *Mirror* soon afterwards. The petition requested that the city "provide an apparatus in order to form a hook and ladder company." The petition asked the Council to visit the ruins of the late fire in order to "take such steps for the protection of life etc. as they deem necessary" (*Florida Mirror*, Sept. 8, 1883). The Council, as before, failed to act but soon learned the high cost of dilatory efforts at fire prevention.

Hardly a week had passed before another disastrous fire occurred. This time the fire was located on the north side of town in the vicinity of the new convent and school of the Sisters of St Joseph, the Mansion House Hotel, the large home of Governor Broome, and all other homes in the neighborhood were threatened. The Dell residence was lost but its contents were saved by "the populous, summoned *en masse*" by the ringing of the bells of the Baptist and Catholic Churches.

Buckets of water to fight the fire were rushed from the well at the Mansion House and from D. M. Hammond's cistern. Men climbed to the rooftops to extinguish the sparks. They hung wet blankets over the windows of the beautiful convent. Despite the heroic efforts of the populace, the Baptist Church was lost. The reporter observed that "all classes and races were represented in fighting the fire....We noticed preachers, colored as well as white, a staid vestryman of the Episcopal Church, merchants, the tall form of a city Alderman, Railroad officials, the portly dimensions of the Collector of Customs, and a prominent contractor.... But all the good work was not confined to the sterner sex. A number of ladies rendered valuable service, especially at the convent, where they gave valuable assistance by carrying water to the men stationed on the roof and elsewhere." The following poignant notice appeared at the end of the *Mirror's* account of the fire: ATTENTION HOOK AND LADDER NUMBER ONE: You are requested to meet at City Council rooms on Monday evening at 8:30 o'clock to perfect an organization and elect officers" (*Florida Mirror*, Sept. 15, 1883).

The City Council, having been made bitterly and abundantly aware of the hazard of fire, ordered once again the re-organization of the Hook and Ladder Company, with officers James McGiffin, foreman; M. N. Gambrill, assistant; and W. F. Wood Jr., secretary and treasurer (*Florida Mirror*, Sept. 22, 1883). On September 24, 1883, the *Mirror* announced that an ordinance establishing a Fire Department "shall be organized by the city of Fernandina…under control of the City Council" (*Florida Mirror*, September 24, 1883).

An editorial in the *Mirror* of October 13, 1883, pointed out the grim opportunity afforded downtown merchants for rebuilding their stores as "handsome buildings," but, this time, made of brick: "We trust no sham veneer work will be done of any kind. Fernandina intends to last too long for that style of architecture."

An ordinance quickly passed to prohibit the building of wooden downtown commercial buildings, and, in addition, the City Council finally committed to provide an official fire department and fire apparatus for the City of Fernandina, underwritten by scrip (a temporary currency issued by the city) at a rate of 8% yearly interest. Each company of firemen was to adopt a uniform (*Florida Mirror*, Dec. 8, 1883). The next week's *Mirror* reported, "Some of our citizens are taking a considerable amount of Fire Department scrip simply as an investment."

Following the calamitous fires, considerable civic pride and enthusiasm for the new Fernandina Fire Department could be read in the pages of the *Mirror*. The paper reported delivery of a new chemical steam engine, ordered from Taylor Manufacturing Company of Chambersburg, Pa. (*Florida Mirror*, Mar. 1, 1884). On March 22, 1884, the *Mirror* proudly announced the exciting arrival of the new chemical fire engine. "The handsome piece of workmanship" was named in honor of Samuel A. Swann, a beloved citizen and prominent businessman. The new fire department conducted a trial of the engine at the baseball grounds, but "owing to the inexperience of the company, the trial was not considered a fair test. It did not bring out the full capacity and effective power of the engine." Notwithstanding the lack of success in the "trial of the engine," the City Council ordered the bill for the *Samuel A. Swann*, in the amount of $1407.80, to "be paid in full" (*Florida Mirror*, Apr. 5, 1884). Sadly, the esteemed Chemical Engine *Samuel A. Swann* also failed a later test in a later Old Town fire. "It was too heavy for the sand" and four buildings were lost (*Florida Mirror*, Nov. 28, 1885).

After the acquisition of the chemical fire engine, it was placed in charge of the Fernandina Chemical Engine Company Number One, an organization of thirty-four members operating under the regulations and ordinances of the city. This organization, the March 22, 1884, *Florida Mirror* reported, split in half with the other half organized once more as the Hook and Ladder Company Number One. James McGiffin was named chief of Fernandina Chemical Engine Company and J. Fred Lohman, foreman. Charles J. Kimball became foreman of Hook and Ladder Company One. The City Council authorized the purchase by the Fire Committee of "two barrels of glass bottles and stoppers for use in the chemical fire engine" (*Florida Mirror*, Dec. 6, 1884).

City fathers enacted even further fire fighting measures. A city ordinance passed requiring "good and substantial ladders, sufficient for approaching every part of a roof" to be placed on all buildings in the city. They ordered fines of $2 to $10 to be levied on homeowners not complying with the ladder ordinance (*Florida Mirror*, May 24, 1884). Old photographs taken from the belvedere of the Egmont Hotel or from the water tower show the ladders were indeed installed on nearly every roof.

Volunteer fire fighter companies supplemented the city's Hook and Ladder Company, including Tiger Hose Company #1 and Tiger Hose, Jr. Horse-drawn tanks of water with long hoses attached were placed in several locations downtown and in a few residential neighborhoods. Volunteers rushed the tanks to the fire on signal from a steam whistle and later from the Courthouse bell that was used for fire alarms and tolled the number of the street on which the fire was located. Volunteers and curious townspeople listened to the number of the street signaled by the bell or whistle

Tiger Hose Co. 1   AIMH

and hurried to the site of the fires. At one time, volunteer firemen were paid $2.50 for each summons to a fire.

After the disastrous fires of 1876 and 1883, the city fathers were faced with the bitter realization that, in spite of the purchase of improved equipment, an abundant water supply and strong pressure were imperative in fighting dangerous fires. Bucket brigades from wells and horse drawn hose and water wagons had proved to be grossly inadequate responses. By 1890, the city had completed a substantial waterworks system, including four miles of iron water mains and fifty fire hydrants. Artesian water flowed through 8-inch pipes, 650 feet deep, discharging 1500 gallons of water per minute. The Chamber of Commerce bragged that the "natural pressure of the water with no mechanical pump would tear shingles from a roof" (*Fernandina/Nassau County, Resources and Advantages,* 1890). In 1891, the Sanborn Insurance map showed the city equipped with two hose carts, a fire alarm tower, electric connections between stations, and forty-five pounds of water pressure.

In his published reminiscences, eighty-four year old Jack McGiffin, from one of Fernandina's prominent Golden Age

By 1892, the city had organized several fire companies and purchased the equipment to better protect its all wood-framed commercial and residential structures.

AIMH

families, recalled his boyhood memories of Fernandina's horse-drawn Hook and Ladder Company equipment. McGiffin described the fire wagons as having solid rubber tires and "the bottoms [of the wagons] were double and in the space between were stowed tools, such as fire axes, bars, etc." He continued:

When I lived in Fernandina [he moved with his family to Jacksonville in 1914] the fire department was horse drawn....We didn't call them fire engines, they were fire wagons. Every morning at daybreak, the alarm would sound in the firehouse and the horses would be backed in place, the harness dropped over them and buckled and off they would go at a full gallop down Second Street all the way to the North end and galloped all the way back to the fire station....I was told it was to exercise the horses so they could be trained and ready."

Update

For many years, the city fire department was housed in City Hall on the corner of South Second and Ash Street. In 1976, Fire Station Number Two was opened on the corner of John S. Robas Road and Glenn Beugnet Street. On July 9, 1996, the fire department moved into a new and more centrally located facility at 225 South Fourteenth Street. The facility was dedicated to the memory of City Commissioner Eleanor Coleman.

AIMH

Nassau County's 1891-92 courthouse replaced previous courthouses located on 2nd Street, at Evergreen and on King's Road between Hilliard and Callahan.

Making a Modern City

The Courthouse

U ntil the present courthouse was built in 1892, Nassau County officials rented office space in downtown buildings, and court was held in the Lyceum, a building on Centre Street where performances and social events took place. Great care was given to the planning stages of the new courthouse building. A Fernandina delegation traveled to Green Cove Springs and Orlando to study the layout and structural plans of their recently built county courthouses. The delegation was impressed, and, as a result, Nassau County officials hired the architect of Clay County's courthouse, A. E. McClure of Jacksonville, and approved nearly identical plans. Nassau County Commission minutes show that bids by several contractors were initially all rejected. W. H. Mann, a local contractor, submitted three bids in succession; his fourth bid of $20,614 won the contract.

The new building featured eleven rooms, including a grand jury room, two petit jury rooms, a County Commission room, Board of Health and Board of Public instruction rooms, a sheriff's office, and a thirty-five by forty-five foot armory. The Clark & Loftus Company won the bid for furniture for $2,050, excluding chairs that were provided by J. W. Mason & Co.

The city fathers determined that December 16, 1891, would be the ceremonial laying of the cornerstone of the Nassau County courthouse. A marble stone was ordered engraved with that date, but in the end the ceremony was postponed. Notwithstanding its incorrect date, the cornerstone was laid on April 12, 1892, and the day was filled with great ceremony and celebration. The next day, the *Florida Times Union* reported the event in glowing terms and called the ceremony "a red letter day in the history of Fernandina:"

Crowds arrived on every train, and by noon the streets were filled with a surging mass of humanity waiting for the parade....The stores, residences, and all the shipping in the harbor were decorated with bunting and flowers and every wagon and carriage had one or more flags fluttering in the breeze." The Island City Band led a fine procession composed of the police, the Masons, the hook and ladder companies, not to mention the "county and state officials, city officials and members of the old Fernandina Volunteers. The four hose carriages and the hook and ladder truck were simply a moving mass of flowers, that of No. 1 being particularly pretty as a result of the efforts of the [Presbyterian] King's Daughters....The new courthouse is to be a beautiful setting, costing about $25,000.

The new courthouse featured cast iron columns and a balcony, topped with a fine tower and steeple. The building's final cost was $25,036, a cost over-run of approximately $5000 from W. H. Mann's original bid. The balcony was a favorite place for speeches, including a noted appearance by William Jennings Bryan. Meneely and Company of West Troy, New York, cast the courthouse bell in 1889, before the ground breaking for the new courthouse had taken place. The bell is described as having a "small town tone." Until the 1930's the bell was a part of the fire alarm system of Fernandina. Cast iron boxes on telephone poles in each neighborhood would set off a simple code connected to ring the courthouse bell. For many years after World War I, the bell tolled at eleven o'clock each morning in commemoration of the Armistice signed at eleven a.m. on November 11, 1918, honoring the memory of those who lost their lives in the conflict. Derrick Kinner, interviewed for a *Times Union* article on Oct. 12, 1993, recalled that in the 1920s a candidate running for Congress had his stump speech interrupted by the bell's chimes. With great aplomb, he immediately began reciting the poem "In Flanders Field the Poppies Grow."

In 1974, a team from the Historic American Buildings Survey labeled the Nassau County courthouse as "typical of courthouse buildings of the era." Although "typical," it was also cited as "unquestionably the finest in quality and detail of all the Victorian courthouse structures still standing in the State of Florida."

Update

In 1953, a bland, utilitarian addition was added to the west side of the courthouse building. In 1977, the Nassau County Commissioners decided to remove the courthouse's deteriorating tower, the most distinctive feature of the building. After an impassioned battle with county commissioners, the tower was extensively repaired through the leadership of the Amelia Island Fernandina Restoration Foundation, although the balcony could not be saved ("Centennial Celebration, Nassau County Courthouse, 1892-1992," pamphlet.). A clock surround adorned the courthouse tower when it was built, but a clock was not installed until the 1977 restoration.

In 1990, the Magnolia Garden Club commissioned an electronic mechanism to be placed on the clock to restore the beloved sound of the courthouse bell striking the daylight hours. The battle to keep the courthouse in repair and functioning as a true courthouse went on for several decades between preservationists and recalcitrant county commissioners from off the island. The commissioners were deaf to outcries from distressed and frustrated citizens that repairs to their cherished building were never made and refused to take action on orders from judges to update safety features and handicap access. Because a handicapped principal in one of his cases could not access the second floor courtroom, a defiant Nassau County judge ordered a tent erected in the street outside of the courthouse and held court there. As a result of the acrimonious struggle of "shiny new" against "cherished old," a meticulous restoration has returned the beautiful old courthouse to its original splendor. At present, the courthouse functions as a civil court and houses offices for the County Clerk of Court and other county services.

The Fernandina Metropolitan Band.

AIMH

The Newport of the South

Social Life of the Golden Age

D
uring Amelia Island's Golden Age years, it is as if pictures of the island's social activities spring forth from the pages of the *Florida Mirror* that report the busy social lives of Fernandina's citizens. Go back to that time, open the pages of the *Mirror* and in your mind's eye *see* the pictures. Turn the pages and imagine strolling down an oak-canopied street; tipping your hat to neighbors including Florida mogul David L. Yulee and journalist, historian, and educator George Rainsford Fairbanks. In the river breeze, watch Jay Gould's fine yacht sail into port. Stroll on the verandah of the Egmont Hotel at a ball honoring a former president of the United States. Dance in orange blossom fragrance under the romantic glow of Chinese lanterns. Take your pick of masque balls, Germans, hops and dances, or enjoy a play or an opera at the Lyceum. With friends, play whist, charades, join a cooking club, have a skating party, go sailing on the river, watch horse races on the beach, attend county fairs, play tennis, go bowling, shoot skeet, go hunting, have seining parties, cheer a championship baseball team, enjoy May Day festivities. Sweet belle epoch, Amelia Island's Golden Age!

As in most small communities, the Amelia Island churches were centers of social life. The *Mirror* often reported Sunday school excursions to the beach or St Marys, Christmas parties, Easter egg hunts, and amateur talent programs at the Lyceum. Boating parties to Dungeness on Cumberland Island appeared to have been so popular with church groups that they may have prompted owner Thomas Carnegie to place several advertisements in the *Mirror* warning that excursions to Dungeness, without permission, would no longer be allowed.

Temporal entertainment abounded. On December 8, 1883, the *Florida Mirror* reported "the monotony of our town is broken now and then by a dance, an oyster roast, a sociable, a horserace, and then another dance!" The Lyceum Hall and the Egmont Hotel were the scenes of many social activities. A reader of the *Mirror* might almost hear the delighted laughter and applause as a Lyceum audience watched neighbors in amateur musicals, or gasps of amazement as a traveling magician performed on the stage. At the elegant Egmont, members and guests of the Comus Club danced the night away to the "entrancing strains of Subert's orchestra." To the dance, Miss Lizzie Jeffreys wore an "empire gown of light blue satin" and Miss Bessie Swann wore "cream crepe and lace" amidst decorations "the finest ever seen." The "Concordia Social Club" also sponsored a "Grand Masque Ball." Not all the dances were grand affairs at the Egmont. On occasion, young and old of Amelia Island danced in moonlit sea breezes near the east wall of deactivated Fort Clinch.

When dancing was not the order of the day, the *Mirror* reported a variety of club activities. An Archery Club met in Egmont Park. "Young ladies and gentlemen" were members of a Riding Club. On January 4, 1879, the *Mirror* reported that the Village Swallows Cooking Club met at the home of Mrs. David Yulee. Forty members were present, all wearing white caps and aprons (*Florida Mirror,* Jan. 4, 1879). Two weeks later, the Club met again, this time at the home of Mrs. W. C. B. Duryee. At the meeting, "an impromptu charade" produced "considerable merriment." The Hibernia Club met at headquarters above the Centre Street store of the Irish Mularkey Brothers, and a Leiderkranz Club represented the German citizenry. Arthur Steil was president and J. Klarer, secretary. The club enjoyed "a very pleasant entertainment" (*Florida Mirror*, Mar. 26, 1882). A later edition of the *Mirror*, on October 4, 1884, described a German-American Citizen's

AIMH

BOOM-STRUCK **FERNANDINA** BROOM-STRUCK.

A Most Unique, Recherche and Enjoyable

ENTERTAINMENT

Will be given the Citizens of Fernandina by

Company A Assisted by Company B,

Fernandina Volunteers

New Year's Eve, Dec. 31, 1886,

When it is intended to

Watch the Old Year Out, and the New Year in.

The principal features of the occasion will be

An Exhibition Drill, by Company A,

Wherein will be executed beautiful and difficult fancy movements, in addition to the Manual.

THE LADIES will then flourish their favorite weapons in a most spirit-stirring

Pfriemenkrautdrillbohrer,

(If you want to know what that is, come and see.)

After which Both Companies will join in a BATALLION DRILL!

131

Club as "semi-social, semi-political." Proceeds from ice cream socials, "pound," and "mite" parties benefited church projects of various denominations. George Wolff assessed fines at a "Poverty Social" where an oyster supper was served with "bivalves in all styles" (*Florida Mirror*, Jan. 17, 1896).

The wife of merchant prince H. E. Dotterer was the "cheerful and untiring president" of the Fernandina Social Club, a club made up of "ladies and gentlemen of the best society." "Refined social intercourse" was the object of the club, according to the *Mirror* of January 20, 1883. Twice monthly, members were required to submit an original journal entry under a *nom de plume* for possible publication in the *Florida Mirror*. The following journals were submitted: Mr. E. S. Loomis—"The Chameleon," Miss Mary Brownson—"The Social Scrap Bag," and Miss Kate Williams—" The Ocean Zephyr." A piece entitled "Fernandina in 1883," submitted by an anonymous author, predicted that Fernandina's City Hall would have fifteen stories; the Lyceum would seat several

Relaxing at the north beach are Angel Davis and friends.

AIMH

thousand; and there would be 150 hotels on the beach. "New York now sends to Fernandina for her supplies" the author concluded (*Florida Mirror*, Mar. 17, 1883). Later journals and poems attributed to club members were also published unsigned.

"For improvement in extempore debating," the *Mirror* reported the organization of a Debating Club. At the second meeting of the club, members considered the subject "Is tobacco smoking injurious to the human body?" (*Florida Mirror*, Nov. 29, 1884). An account of the Roller Skating Club Carnival appeared in the *Florida Mirror* on April 5, 1884: "Masked skaters will be allowed to skate free." In anticipation of the carnival and other Skating Club activities, the *Mirror* reported that a new supply of skates had been ordered from New York, and the Mallory steamship *City of Antonio* delivered the skates in time for the party. Miss Jennie Maxwell and Miss Jennie Taylor appeared at a skating party in costumes made up entirely of copies of the *Mirror* "dotted with little round mirrors" and the *Mirror* reported itself "highly complimented" on January 12, 1884. The Ladies Whist Club met at the home of H. E. Dotterer, reported the *Fernandina News* on January 17, 1896, including Eva Fairbanks, Lizzie Jeffreys, Fannie Williams, Kate Williams, and Bessie Swann.

In addition to club activities, Fernandina residents had many opportunities for sport and recreation. Before the days of the Strathmore Hotel and private cottages on the beach, city investors built a private Bath Club on the river at the foot of Broome Street in 1868. Alice Youngblood, in her research for *Seeing Fernandina*, described the Bath Club as having a floored swimming area, deep on one end, shallow on the other, and fenced with chicken wire. No person was admitted without a yellow ticket supplied to stockholders and their families. Ladies and gentlemen swam on alternate days—on Ladies Day a white flag was raised over the bathhouse. The names of Amelia Island's most prominent families could be found on the list of stockholders: Scott, Roux, Riddell, Noyes, Mann, Dotterer, Freeman, Friend, Hedges, Huot, Kelly, Maxwell, Williams, Baker, Suhrer, Swann, the Reverend Owen P. Thackara, and many others.

Activities at the Atlantic beaches were also popular. Young people gave an "apron and necktie" party at the Lyceum, with proceeds of the entertainment dedicated to "aid in reconstruction of the pavilion on Amelia Beach which was washed away by high tides last fall" (*Florida Mirror,* May 23, 1885). In mullet and whiting season, seining parties on the beach netted hundreds of the silvery fish that were immediately popped into a pan waiting over a fire in the sand, or split and seasoned for hours of slow smoking in backyard ovens. In a day when "endangered species" meant the carrier pigeon and the Carolina parakeet, there were night excursions to the beach to steal eggs from sea turtle nests. Hundreds of ping-pong-like turtle eggs were boiled in red-peppered salty water and eaten by the dozen, especially by the local men who discussed with one another an arcane benefit of eating this coastal delicacy.

Tennis was a favorite sport. Courts at the Marcellus Williams house and at the Yulee house were popular. There were horse races on Amelia Beach, a beach often described as "smooth as a floor." The *Mirror* of January 27, 1883, reported that in a "scrub race" for horses of Nassau County, Mr. Wingate's mare came in the winner and J. J. Acosta's mare was second. The *Mirror* announced that on June 14, 1884, "a trotting race for a $100 purse" had been arranged to take place "in the afternoon at 5 o'clock on Amelia Beach, between two of Tom McMurray's horses of Jacksonville."

Sleek narrow sailboats raced in competition in the river and around the sea buoy. In connection with a Nassau County Fair weekend, the *Mirror*, on May 10, 1879, reported a yacht race in the river "under New York rules." There were three entries, the *Orilla*, sailed by Clay Williams of Brunswick, the *Hattie*, sailed by George Gilcrist, and the *Louise Adele*, sailed by C. Wickliff Yulee. Unfortunately "the *Hattie* tried the overland route and stuck in the mud," the *Mirror* reported.

As part of County Fair weekend activities, the *Mirror* also noted that a Mrs. Lines and a Mrs. Partington had entered the "single skull race" on the river. The ladies, whose first names were not given in the newspaper account, were "well known in the oyster business and were capable of skulling for many miles and for many hours in their line of work." Odds in favor of Mrs. Lines were five to four, but due to threatening weather, the race was called off. Instead, there was a "four oared race" with James Bell in the *Adair* and William LeFils in the *Willie*.

In anticipation of a re-scheduled race between the ladies, the *Mirror*, on June 7, 1879, published an interview with Mrs. Lines, the apparent favorite. During the interview, Mrs. Lines revealed that in the next month she would reach her sixty-ninth birthday. On the day of the interview, Mrs. Lines had rowed from her home, to the fishing grounds, and "thence to town, a distance of 18 miles. After catching and selling her fish, she had rowed back home, in all a distance of 25 miles." The reported concluded, "This is no fish story either." The boat race between the ladies "finally came off in grand style," with a crowd of spectators on the docks and decks of steamers cheering and congratulating the intrepid Mrs. Lines as she won the race. The Old Town Yacht Club announced a sail boat race with the course between the ballast dock on Tiger Island, to the foot of Centre Street, to Tiger

Spit buoy, and back to the line of starting (*Florida Mirror*, Jun. 7, 1879).

Thomas Carnegie's yachts, the *Dream,* the *Wisso,* and the *Skibo,* often visited the Fernandina harbor. Mrs Carnegie's sea-going yacht, the *Dungeness,* was a 119 foot screw schooner that flew the burgee of the New York Yacht Club, since Mrs. Carnegie had the distinction of being the first female member of that prestigious club. "Jay Gould's splendid yacht, the steamship *Atalanta,* returned here and remained in the harbor several days...Fernandina is the only port on the east coast affording sufficient draught for the *Atalanta,* " reported the *Florida Mirror* on March 22, 1884. The *Fernandina Record,* on January 9, 1908, reported a visit to the Fernandina port from the *Garnet* of Philadelphia and the *Azara* of New York, with "cruising parties" aboard: "Our harbor is so large and our waters so pleasant they offer a tempting inducement for a rest to the smaller vessel which has been battling the seas."

Golden Age citizens observed the pageantry of May Day annually around the pool in Central Park. The *Florida Mirror* of June 7, 1884, complimented the city founders for their "great wisdom and forecast" in establishing the park on Centre Street: "It is a place for children to meet and enjoy themselves out of the streets; a place where with proper shade and shelter visitors can find pleasure and recreation; where baby carriages can have ample room, and young folks have somewhere to promenade, and old folks to rest." A delightful old photograph owned by the Amelia Island Museum of History shows beautifully dressed mothers guiding a parade of costumed children past the Lyceum Hall toward the park for May Day festivities.

Much excitement was evident in accounts found in the *Mirror* in February of 1879 regarding Amelia Island exhibits at a Gainesville Fair. According to the *Mirror* of February

22, 1879, German-American Jacob Klarer won a prize for the best blood pudding and bologna sausage. Mr. Linville exhibited paper made from palmetto, and the Artificial Stone Company of Fernandina displayed chimney tops, lawn vases, and well curbings. Mr. J. T. O'Neill exhibited the only celery at the fair. The railroad shops exhibited jacks, stoves, pumps, grate-bars, gearings, tools, and other castings made by their foundry. Mrs. David L. Yulee was presented a "diploma" for an oil painting, and C. Wickliffe Yulee received a "diploma" for a cane woodcarving. The Fernandina Light Infantry entered a target-shooting contest, and won $50 in gold in a drill competition.

Nassau County also had a fair later that year and the *Mirror* gave it extensive coverage in the May 10, 1879, issue. At the fair, Mrs. Gustave Stark exhibited the latest millinery fashions. There were many displays of lace, footrests, slippers, feather fans, pincushions and afghans. The Palmetto Fiber Company displayed palmetto hats. Agricultural products were on display, including strawberries and "a branch of an apple tree bearing six apples."

Baseball was a favorite island sport during the Golden Age. Between the years 1879 and 1900, several local teams were mentioned in the *Mirror's* social columns: the Osceola Baseball Club, the Mechanics Baseball Club—F. Lohman, captain, George Wolff president— the Railroad Nine, the Uptown Boys, and the Island City Baseball club. The Island City uniforms were described in the *Mirror* on September 9, 1882, as "white flannel shirts, knee breeches, red stockings, and derby-style straw hats." J. Fred Lohman served as umpire. The baseball games were played on a field behind what is now the City Hall of Fernandina. The *Florida Mirror*, in June 1883, reported that all the island baseball clubs had consolidated into one organization. The consolidation apparently paid off: The Baseball Club of Fernandina won the title of "Champions of Florida" on September 22, 1894. A hand written, unsigned roster of the winning team, found in the archives of the Amelia Island Museum of History lists the following players and their positions:

Frank Williams	Third Base
Eddie Williams	First Base
J. A. Nix	Pitcher
Johnnie McGiffin	Left Field
Henry Hobein	Utility
Frank Williams	Right Field
Wallace Maxwell	Second Base and Captain

The 1894 Fernandina baseball team.

AIMH

Gussie McDonell	Center Field
Johnny Sauls	Utility
Fritz Hobein	Utility
Charlie Hernandez	Catcher

The social column of the *Mirror* carried long lists of hotel visitors from wide-spread locations each week during tourist season. An item in the December 11, 1878, edition noted that "Professor and Mrs. Harriett Beecher Stowe and two daughters came through Fernandina on their way to their winter home in Mandarin." "Miss Mariana Papy, of Tallahassee, is spending the summer. Her handsome team of grays is much admired." Of no less social interest was the cryptic notation, included in the January 22, 1881, edition of the *Mirror*, that crowds of curious spectators had watched a "double-headed woman" arrive at Centre Street aboard the steamer *Florida*, and walk from the dock to board the train to Jacksonville.

An invitation to the wedding of David Yulee's eldest daughter Margaret to C. H. Reed, Jr, of Washington must have caused no little excitement among Amelia Island's social elite. Under the title, "Hymeneal," the *Florida Mirror*, on April 29, 1882, described "The Marriage of Miss Yulee at Fernandina." The home of the bride's parents at North Third and Alachua Streets where the wedding took place was decorated with "costly and elaborate decorations." "An immense marriage bell, made of white roses, with a tongue of violets was suspended from the arch of a mammoth horseshoe" (*Florida Mirror*, Apr. 15, 1882). "A band stationed in the hall provided wedding music....The bridal party was preceded by six little girls carrying hats filled with flowers, and five bridesmaids in white organdy over white silk *en train*. The bride's dress was of white satin and watered silk trimmed with point lace and embroidered with silk and pearls. Her beautiful veil was fastened with orange blossoms and diamonds." Following the wedding, "an elaborate supper was served in the garden. The grounds were lighted with innumerable Chinese lanterns, the effect being most beautiful...Presents were numerous and costly, but were not displayed." The bride and groom left the island by "special train to begin an extensive bridal tour" *(Florida Mirror,* Apr. 29, 1882).

As impressive as the Yulee wedding was, the zenith of social events in that era was undoubtedly the visit, in January 1880, of Ulysses S. Grant, eighteenth president of the United States. A sense of the community's anticipation and excitement over this momentous occasion is evident in the issues of the *Florida Mirror* published before and after the event:

When it was learned that President Grant and his entourage would pass through Florida on his way to Key West, Cuba, the West Indies, and Mexico, Fernandina's prominent businessmen went into a frenzy of preparation. Committees were appointed to extend an invitation to President Grant to visit Amelia Island and to prepare a suitable reception. Mayor Norman Brownson was chairman of the prestigious committee, and Samuel A. Swann, Esquire, and retired Confederate General W. G. M. Davis were members *(Florida Mirror,* December 31, 1879).

The *Florida Mirror* of January 3, 1880, also reported the enthusiastic participation of the black community in celebrating Grant's visit. Under the heading, "Colored Reception to General Grant," the *Mirror* reported: "The Young Benevolent Association and I. O. & O. F. have appointed the following committees to take the necessary steps for welcoming General Grant to the city. Arrangements: Walter

Davis, B. Holland, Robert McDonell, Louden Dumfield, and Roman Cribb. Reception: J. R. Ballard, W. J. Brookens, Riley E. Robinson, H. B. Delaney, W. C. Cole, Benjamin Holland, Mary Francis and Charlotte Eddin. Address: J. R. Ballard, E. J. Brookens, and Riley E. Robinson."

Excitement heightened when Fernandina Mayor Norman Brownson received the following telegram signed by F. D. Grant, the general's son: "Will leave Savannah on Saturday's boat and you can fix time for the reception of General Grant." Major W. B. C. Duryee and Captain C. Wickliffe Yulee were dispatched to Savannah to meet the General, "ascertain his plans, and to facilitate his movement."

The *Florida Mirror* of January 14, 1880, described Grant's visit. "A large concourse of citizens met the *City of Bridgeton* on which the General had sailed from Brunswick. At the dock, the Honorable David L. Yulee gave a brief greeting of welcome, then the General's party, consisting of the General,

Leisurely past times of 1885.

Florida Memory Project
Florida Department of State
PR 03031

his wife, her maid, General and Mrs. Sheridan, Colonel F. D. Grant and his wife, and several others, were escorted to the Egmont where the rest of the afternoon was devoted to rest and refreshments." At five o'clock, Generals Grant and Sheridan and others enjoyed "quietly and keenly" a drive on the beach.

That night, in a setting handsomely illuminated with Chinese lanterns, the Brunswick Brass Band, which had accompanied the general's party from Brunswick, "discoursed sweet music upon the soft night air. The splash of water in the fountains of the park and the solemn roaring of the distant sea mingling with the strains of music from the land seemed to have a restful and soothing effect on the distinguished travelers who retired early to their comfortable rooms."

On Monday morning a reception was held in the

Grant's visit to Cumberland Island

"handsomely and tastefully" decorated City Hall, and officials offered the general and his party the hospitality of the city. Speeches of welcome and speeches of reply were made and "three hearty cheers went up for General Grant, and three for General Sheridan." A deputation of members from a black temperance society presented an address to which General Grant graciously replied, "encouraging them in temperance reform."

The General, his party, and invited guests then boarded the steamer *Florence* for a cruise to Cumberland Island and Dungeness, where they viewed the ruins of the mansion of General Nathaneal Greene and visited the grave of Lighthorse Harry Lee, father of General Robert E. Lee. On their return to Fernandina, "a recently captured Bald Eagle was presented to the General" by a Colonel Styles. In response, the General "expressed the hope that the American people would imitate in politics the flight of this able bird soaring high above all national strife and difficulties." Over a hundred years later, it is to be devoutly wished that the General freed the eagle before continuing his journey, just as he had magnanimously freed David Yulee, Fernandina's premier citizen, from Fort Pulaski prison. As the *Florence* passed Fort Clinch, a booming salute to the General was fired from the ramparts.

"An occasion of unalloyed pleasure" described the ball held on their return that night at the Egmont *(Florida Mirror,* January 14, 1880):

An elegant collation was spread in the gentlemen's parlor which was decorated with evergreen, tropical plants, flags, and flowers....On the handsome lambrequins of the windows was the name 'U. S. Grant' in large letters formed of pure white camellias brought from Tallahassee as a gift from Mr. F. B. Papy....The camellias were placed in every available position....The first quadrille at the reception contained a set composed of the following couples: General Grant and Mrs. David L. Yulee; General Sheridan and Miss Acklin; Honorable D. L. Yulee and Mrs. Grant; General Davis and Mrs. Grant.

The bitterness between Confederate and Yankee, at least for this magical occasion, yielded to good will and high spirits.

The morning after the ball, the General and his party departed Fernandina on a special train. "The Fernandina Light Artillery in full dress uniform with two twelve-pounders fired a salute of 21 guns as the train moved off amid the cheers and good wishes of a large assemblage of citizens." The gracious salute and cheers for Grant must have contrasted greatly with what, only a few years before, would have been well-aimed artillery and jeers. "Taken altogether," the *Mirror* declared, "the affair may be considered in all respects a most brilliant

A 1907 fishing party brought several hundred pounds of reds and grouper.

Florida Memory Project
Florida Department of State
RC 07574

The Newport of the South

Fernandina's Hotels

The early hotels of Amelia Island were by-products of David Yulee's cross-state railroad. In 1857, to accommodate the railroad's eastern terminus, the new town of Fernandina was a-building, and housing had to be provided for construction workers. The Pioneer Hotel, owned by Mr. Amaziah Coy, appears in the Methodist Church records of 1855, and it is probable that Mr. Coy's Pioneer Hotel is the same one described in a letter found among the papers of Samuel A. Swann. In this letter, written from Armour, South Carolina, on May 2, 1903, Henry M. Drane set down his memories of the very earliest days of new Fernandina for Samuel Swann's brother Jim: "I think the first house built at Fernandina was the old 'Coy Hotel'. When I first landed there...the Coy House was then either finished or nearly so and there was no other building there." Drane is referring to the dearth of buildings in "New Fernandina," site of the terminus of the railroad, not the "Old Town" settlement that extends back to the days of Spanish Florida.

The Florida House, still in business at 20 and 22 South Third Street, is probably the oldest hotel in the state of Florida. The inn shared its birth date with the new town of Fernandina, since trustees of the Florida Railroad built the original wing of the building in 1857. In 1869, Major and Mrs. Thomas Leddy purchased the Florida House. Major Leddy had served with the "Fighting Irish" 69th Regiment of New York State Volunteers, and settled in Fernandina in 1865 as Provost Marshal of Northern Florida. After Major Leddy's death, his widow Anne, with the help of her sisters Charlotte

PARTIN FAMILY COLLECTION

Suzanne Hardee

FLORIDA HOUSE..

......Leading Hotel of......

Fair Fernandina

CENTRALLY LOCATED,

...Third Street, South of Centre...

and Maria, ran the inn for fifteen years. The *Florida Mirror*, on November 4, 1882, reported that the Florida House had been enlarged "with an addition to the north consisting of 12 rooms." *Webb's Historical and Industrial and Biographical History of Florida*, published in 1885, described the Florida House: "Without seeming to be watched or patronized, guests are looked after with kindness and affection. There is no more cozy or homelike place for the weary and hungry in all of Florida than this modest, airy, pleasantly located hotel." The Florida House later operated for decades as a rooming house and apartments, but new owners restored the fine old building and returned it to its original role as one of Fernandina's most popular inns.

A hotel named "The Virginia House" was also known to be in existence in Fernandina before 1868. This information is found in a copy of an advertisement found in the archives of the Amelia Island Museum of History, but, to date, little is known of this hotel.

The fifty-room Mansion House was another of Fernandina's oldest hotels, opened in 1871 shortly after the end of Union occupation. The Mansion House was located on Broome Street, facing north, between Third and Fourth Streets. Newspaper advertisements of the day stated that the Mansion was "well known to the traveling public...near the steamer docks and the depot." Colonel M. W. Downie served as its proprietor (*Florida Mirror*, Dec. 7, 1878). The Mansion House was described in the *Florida Mirror* on January 3, 1880, as having arched drawing rooms that had a quiet elegance that pleased "world wide tourists." *Webb's History* of *Florida* called the Mansion House "a popular caravansary...a Mecca of commercial travelers...50 elegantly appointed rooms furnished in walnut and cherry...completely renovated and refurbished...hot and cold baths, electric bells, and orange trees all around, with a parterre of flowers."

In February 1884, the porch of the Mansion House became notorious as the scene of the fatal shooting of the prominent and highly respected manager of the hotel, Fernando C. Suhrer. Suhrer, a native of the Duchy of Baden in Germany, had served as a Union army officer in the Civil War. In 1866, he acted as postmaster of the City of Fernandina and, at the time of his death, was president of the City Council of Fernandina. Suhrer was shot by Thomas Jefferson Epps, a conductor on the Florida Peninsular Railroad, and son of Judge J. T. Epps of Monticello, Florida. Epps, newly married, had accused Suhrer of "insulting my wife." Suhrer, facing Epps's loaded weapon, was said to have replied, "I may be a dead man but before God, I did not" (*Florida Mirror*, Feb. 9, 1884). Fernandina was outraged over the shooting. The *Mirror* reported receiving "several communications bearing on the case but we deem it best the case should be tried in the court and not in newspapers." Due to the prominence of Suhrer and Epps, the venue of what would be a sensational jury trial was moved to neighboring Duval County (*Florida Mirror*, Apr, 26, 1884). Epps was acquitted and apparently survived socially unscathed. A notation, on September 19, 1885, in the "Reflections" column of the *Florida Mirror* mentioned that "Conductor T. Jeff Epps has gone to Hendersonville, North Carolina to join his family and the colony of Fernandina people."

One of Fernandina's favorite ghost stories stems from this tragic shooting. It is said that the ghost of the beautiful "insulted wife" still haunts one of Fernandina's fine old residences. She weeps and wrings her hands in sorrow that her mischievous accusation, made to evoke the jealously and attention of her own handsome husband, instead cost the life of Fernando Suhrer, faithful husband and father of six. Many friends mourned Suhrer's death. At his funeral, "Many a strong man, to whom tears had been strangers for years, was seen to weep" *(Florida Mirror*, Feb. 16, 1884). An anonymous donor sent $3 to the widowed Mrs. Suhrer *(Florida Mirror*, Feb. 23, 1884). The Mansion House, scene of the crime, burned in February 1887.

Older residents of Amelia Island remember the Albemarle Hotel, a large wooden hotel on Broome Street between Fourth and Fifth Streets, with wide porches and a distinctive mansard roof. First called the Norwood House, the hotel became the Tourist Hotel in 1883. Sidney Lanier mentioned the Norwood House in his book *Florida, Its Scenery and Climate and History*, published in 1875. It is not known

The Albemarle Inn was on Broome Street between 4th and 5th Streets North. It catered heavily to sea captains and other port related visitors.

SWANN / CARROLL COLLECTION - AIMH

when the Norwood House or Tourist Hotel became known as the Albemarle. Turned into apartments, the Albemarle stood, a faded beauty, until the 1960s when it was torn down.

The Riddell House was the second of the Fernandina hotels listed by Sidney Lanier. The Riddell House was on Fifth Street between Broome and Calhoun and was the principal hotel of the city until the Egmont Hotel opened for guests in 1878.

Samuel T. Riddell was mayor of Fernandina during the years 1875-1878 and served as postmaster in 1879. In 1883, George M. Barbour, correspondent of the *Chicago Times* reported that the Riddell and Mansion Houses were "spacious, and well kept, all crowded during the season."

The third hotel mentioned by Lanier was the Egmont House, but his reference to the Egmont House is a mystery to local historians who have no knowledge of the Egmont *House*. The famous Egmont *Hotel* was not built until two years after Lanier's book was published.

Boarding houses, of which there were many, were often advertised in the local newspapers. The following list of boarding house proprietors is from *Webb's Florida, Fernandina Directory*, 1887 edition:

Bache, Charles W.	Fourth and Ash
Caldwell, Catherine	Beech and Fifth
Cowell, ?	Beech and Fifth
Hudson, P.J	Fourth and Ash
Hunt, Lorna, Mrs.	Fifth and Ash
Krues, Fred, Mrs.	First and Ash
Thompson, Lucy, Mrs.	Seventh Street
Tavel, Elizabeth, Mrs.	Fifth Street
Tucker, Ruth, Mrs.	Third and Centre.
T.M. Burbank	Location Unknown

Miller House	Fourth and Calhoun
Jacob Miller Property	Location Unknown

Of the above list, Lucy Cottage, Mrs. Thompson's boarding house at 17 Seventh Street, was the most prominently advertised. It was described in the *Florida Mirror* of December 8, 1883, as a "First Class Boarding House...A pleasant place for tourists, recently opened by Miss Lucy O. Thompson...a pretty cottage on Seventh Street. Newly furnished in a most complete and cozy manner. Lucy Cottage, as it has been happily named, will prove a valuable accession." Until her death in August of 1999, the namesake of the original Lucy lived in Lucy Cottage on South Seventh Street.

The undisputed queen of Amelia Island hotels was the elegant Egmont. The Egmont was built at the behest of David Yulee with the financial involvement of the Florida Railroad. The Egmont, Florida's first real tourist hotel, became the showpiece of "the Newport of the South." Building was begun in 1877 and completed in 1878 at a cost of $150,000. The four-story hotel stretched 134 feet on Seventh Street and 128 feet along Beech. The belvedere-adorned structure contained sixty-five sleeping apartments and elegant dining facilities for one hundred guests. There were gas lights, steam heat, hot and cold water, telephone and telegraph connections on each floor, hairdressing rooms, and a news and curiosity shop which dispensed all leading dailies and periodicals and souvenirs. There were fireplaces in every room, baths on every floor, communication tubes called "Creighton oral annunciators," fire hoses, and elaborate gardens and fountains. According to the *Florida Mirror* of January 28, 1881, all this could be had for $2.50 or $3.00 per day.

During the season of 1880, the Egmont entertained over one thousand guests. The *Florida Mirror,* not wholly objective since it was also a Yulee-influenced institution, stated that "the Egmont is the pride of the city—yes, pride of the State—a princely home for tourists" (*Florida Mirror*, Feb. 18, 1880). A year later, the paper exclaimed that "The elite of the land and the most fastidious are delighted with this gem of a hotel" (*Florida Mirror*, Mar. 5, 1881). Courteous porters met every boat and train coming to the island and transported guests to the hotel in fine Egmont coaches. In addition to a splendid bill of fare, guests could chose from an incredible mélange of recreational activities. Guests could be entertained by tennis, rowing, sailing, fishing, hunting, skeet, croquet, archery, a shooting gallery, a bowling alley, billiards, steam yacht rides to Cumberland Island, and trolley rides to the beach. A "beautiful pleasure steamer," especially constructed for the Egmont Hotel, was another source of entertainment for pampered guests. The *Florida Mirror* on January 20, 1882, described the steamer as sixty feet in length with a draft of three feet. There was seating for one hundred people on the steamer's awning-covered decks and a "bunker room" for six tons of coal. "One man can steer her, stop, start and back her engines with perfect ease." Captain G. F. Harding was in charge.

Webb's Florida praised the Egmont's lovely gardens that could be viewed from wrap-around porches on the first and second stories: "Opposite the hotel is a beautiful orange-palmetto park for the exclusive use of its guests, and the space between the hotel and the street to the rear is converted into a finely appointed garden handsomely decorated with parterres of flowers, fountains, etc." From the belvedere, the Egmont guests enjoyed a panoramic view of the harbor and ocean, an ideal place to view the sunset over the river, described by one guest as "watching the large orb as red as a ball of fire sink into the ground back of the trees with color as would baffle the efforts of the best artist" (*Florida Mirror*, Mar. 22, 1884). A "Winter Pilgrim, from the country of ice and snows and sleety storms," described the atmosphere of the hotel grounds as "fragrant with a thousand flowers, orange, lemon, pomegranate, fig, date, and banana." With even more effusion and imagination, the Pilgrim reported: "In December roses are blushing profusely, the sweet violets shade the grass into purple, and the stately camellias, Spanish bayonets and the lily bursts into a thousand hues while waving plumes of the date palm, and banana are responsive to the breeze whose waves are like the zephyrs of Arabia (*Florida Mirror*, Mar. 4, 1879). Mr. Leopold Beugnet, the Egmont's "new florist," was complimented in the *Florida Mirror* of October 25, 1879 for the hotel's beautiful grounds and gardens.

A fine copy of a portrait of Catharine, the dowager Countess of Egmont and her two-year-old son, Charles Perceval, hung in the principal drawing room of the Egmont Hotel. The Countess was the daughter of Charles Compton, Earl of Northhampton. The painting was described in a brief article that was copied from the *Florida Times Union* in the *Florida Mirror* issue of April 26, 1884. The article noted that Catharine had been "created Baroness of Arden in her own right," and credited her with "establishing an indigo plantation on Amelia Island about 1770."

The first proprietor of the Egmont was Captain Samuel Skinner, who had previously worked at the famous Palmer House in Chicago. The *Florida Mirror*, in its many articles relating to the Egmont, was generous in describing Skinner's professionalism. He trained "hotel servants from the north" to a superlative degree. Female employees were labeled as "attractive interesting Saxon girls." *The Mirror* praised Skinner for a bill of fare which was the "most elegant and artistic ever spread on a table in Florida." "From basement to attic was found cultivated and refined taste." An article in the *Florida Mirror* on November 30, 1878, reported that Captain Sam P. Skinner had received his trotting horse "Shoo Fly" on the last steamer. "He may be seen on the beach every fine afternoon." Skinner's health, however, soon failed, and, in 1880, A. L. Mellen, former proprietor of the Royal Victoria, Nassau, assumed management of the Egmont. Other proprietors mentioned in the *Mirror* were Mr. F. B. Papy, Mr. George W. Kittelle, Mr. Lukenbill, Mr. William P. Davis, and Mr. L. F. Goodsell, a "well known hotel keeper

The Florida Mirror - AIMH

The Egmont Hotel.

WM. P. DAVIS, Proprietor,   *FERNANDINA, FLA.*

Elegantly furnished and equipped with all the modern improvements, inclusive of gas, steam heat, coal or wood fires, annunciators in sleeping-rooms, hot and cold water baths, etc., on every floor, telegraph and telephone connection with all points. Billiards, Bowling and Lawn Tennis have been provided for the amusement of the guests.

AIMH

of Cozzens Hotel below West Point" (*Florida Mirror*, Oct. 16, 1881). The death of James Murray, head porter of the Egmont, was reported in the *Florida Mirror* on May 3, 1879. Murray was described as a "true nobleman" and "his coffin was literally buried in flowers."

The *Florida Mirror* published a weekly guest list, and names from the social registers of the largest cities of the United States and abroad stand out, including architect Sanford White and wife, Jay Gould, Edwin Gould, General James Longstreet, Mrs. Gould and Mrs. Tiffany, T. T. Snow, wife, child, and servant, Dr. J. J. Mason and wife of Newport, Rhode Island, the Duke of Castellwick, the Earl of Huntington, and Lord Hastings from England. The frequent "Newport of the South" designation was not merely an idle boast. The *Florida Mirror* reported on January 25, 1879, that "quite a number of families from New York and Chicago, and Boston, are already located at the Egmont for the winter season." At times the hotel was so full, "clients had to be accommodated in private homes."

Weekly hops, often decorated with Chinese lanterns, were held at the Egmont each Wednesday night with "guests of the right sort—jovial and happy" (*Florida Mirror*, Mar. 22, 1879). At the hops, the "soft plaintive music of the Egmont String Band fell on the midnight air with the dull roar of the ocean heard in the background."

McAvoy's Band, sometimes called the Juvenile Band, played for Egmont guests. The band, "led by an "imperturbable" local boy named Pumpkin, did not receive rave reviews in the *Mirror* of March 1, 1879: "Their instruments need voicing, especially the tin oil can which serves as a drum." A more kindly reporter, writing for *Harper's New Monthly Magazine* on November 1878, wrote: "I was often amused by a rustic musical band which used to come to the hotel of an evening to earn a few pennies by drumming on boxes and blowing tin trumpets. If there was not much music in the performance there was certainly a rhythm in the stroke and a prodigious earnestness in the efforts of the young musicians. Pumpkin, the smallest of them, was a character." "Listen to the Mockingbird" was a favorite rendition. McAvoy's Band appears to have been named for the Honorable John H. McAvoy of Chicago, who spent the winters of 1878 and 1879 at the Egmont and was a great fan of the ragtag band's performances. The *Florida Mirror* of March 29, 1879, labeled McAvoy the "patron saint of Pumpkin's Tin Band."

Guests with possibly more refined tastes could enjoy a "Parlor Concert" such as the one reported in the *Florida Mirror*, March 22, 1884. Concert guests enjoyed the "recherché programme" rendered by the Egmont's orchestra that consisted of a cornet, violin, and piano. At the concert, Major W. B. C. Duryee, prominent local businessman, sang "a well chosen solo." Providing more musical sophistication, Madame E. deBarry of New York, a professional pianist, was engaged to entertain guests of the hotel. Madame deBarry "a widely known composer and pianist" according to the *Mirror* of January 13, 1883, would "take pupils on the side."

The gowns of local belles attending an Egmont ball were often described in glowing detail in the *Florida Mirror*: "Miss Jennie McGiffin wore terra cotta cashmere and silk ribbons; Miss Stark, cream albatross and silk; Miss Lucy Thompson, white silk and lace; Miss Hillyer, white cashmere and passementerie."

In those un-air conditioned days, the Egmont season closed in the spring. "Swallows homeward fly," announced the *Florida Mirror* at the end of the 1879 season. "The steamers are loaded to the decks with departing guests. The Egmont still has 40 or 50 guests. It looks as if it's a pleasure to linger." On May 3, 1879, an article in the *Mirror* reported the "Exodus" that finally finished the season:

> The entire force of Saxon girls and servants led by the head porter marched through the hall and headed to the water loaded down with all sorts of Florida productions. Jim, most courteous of courteous head-waiters, had a basket of shells on each arm and cages of birds and live alligators strapped before and behind.... They marched down the street to the *Tybee* on which they took passage to New York.

The marvelous Egmont's colorful history was sadly short-lived. Her demise was slow but very sure. By 1895, fickle visitors from the north had discovered the more elaborate Flagler and Plant hotels in Saint Augustine and Tampa. David Yulee's railroad had gone into receivership, and Fernandina's Golden Age was in decline. In 1899, Samuel Swann, one of the original railroad tycoons, revealed that the Egmont Hotel structure that had cost $150,000 to build could be bought for $3,000. In 1900, the Egmont was sold to Swann for $2,100. Swann tried to promote alternative uses of the building such as a cigar factory, a sportsman's club, or a girls' school. He attempted to sell the fading beauty to Henry Flagler, but the death knell of the Egmont had tolled. In 1905, Louis Hirth, local entrepreneur, bought the rapidly deteriorating building and the hotel, sadly, was torn down, but Hirth used the fine lumber of the hotel to build four identical houses on the west side of Seventh Street between Beech and Ash and three cottages behind them on South Sixth Street. The fish pools, once a part of the beautiful Egmont gardens, now lie hidden beneath the residence at 130 South Seventh Street.

The Newport of the South
The Lyceum

A"Lyceum" is defined as a hall for public lectures, concerts, and entertainment. Fernandina's Lyceum Hall stood mid-block on the south side of Centre Street, between Sixth and Seventh Streets. It was a plain utilitarian building, built in 1873 by the Fernandina Lyceum Association, but for decades, it was the center of secular community activities on Amelia Island.

Captain George T. Davis presented original documents of the organization of the Association to the Amelia Island Museum of History. These documents, dated November 29, 1872, show that the Association was established with a capital stock, at $100 a share, of $4000. Original principals of the Association were listed as follows: "H. E. Dotterer, George Dewson, Samuel A. Swann, W. N. Thompson, John Hedges, Thomas Kydd, and G. Stark." The Association purchased property for their new building from Louis Coxetter of Charleston, South Carolina. The object of the Association was "to build public halls or lyceums in the city of Fernandina." The forward-looking principals of the Association used the plural of lyceums and halls "in case tastes and necessities of the people and citizens shall require and demand the erection and construction of *other* public halls and buildings." John Hedges was listed as president of the Association in the *Florida Mirror* of April 23, 1881. Two years later, it was noted in the *Mirror* of June 30, 1883, that the Association had declared a 7% dividend.

"A Winter Pilgrim," in a letter to the *Florida Mirror* of January 25, 1879, wrote: "You have told us of the beauty of Fernandina and the charms of Nature, but pray, after you get us there what are you going to do with us?" The Lyceum answered the question by offering an amazing variety of entertainment both to residents and to hotel guests who flocked to Amelia Island for winter sojourns. Hotel and boarding-house guests, incredibly, could find themselves enjoying the same caliber of entertainment at the Lyceum that they experienced back home at theaters in cities far larger than Fernandina. For decades, advertisements and reviews of Lyceum entertainment were regularly reported in the *Florida Mirror*. Noted professional singers and actors of the time performed in many operas and plays, including the operas *Martha* and *Cavalleria Rusticana,* and the dramas *Jane Eyre, The Little Minister, Ten Nights in a Bar Room, The Wife's Peril, Rip Van Winkle, The Count of Monte Cristo,* and many others.

Minstrel shows, medicine shows, and Swiss Bell Ringers also delighted audiences. Professor J. M. MacAllister, Wizard of the World, performed "wonderful, startling feats of prestidigitation." "Blind Tom…the musical phenomenon of the age, the greatest pianist living" returned to the Lyceum each year to entertain and amaze the audience with his ability to play any piece of music "merely by hearing it one time." In 1889, when memories of Fernandina's similar epidemic were fresh, a ventriloquist performed for the benefit of victims of the "late yellow fever epidemic in Mobile."

In operettas, talent shows, musicals, and plays, local talent also flourished on the kerosene-lamp-lit Lyceum stage. Major W. B. C. Duryee was often a featured vocalist. In the *Mirror* of May 24, 1879, a "Spectator" effusively reported the production of a *Floral Cantata*:

Real life was forgotten for once, and as if by the touch of a fairy's wand, the most prosaic soul was captured will or nill, and floated under the greenwood tree, there to frolic with the daintiest and most graceful set of elves that ever danced to woodland song.... Roses without thorns, lilies without spot, crocuses and mignonette and baby-kneed heather-bells had taken possession of shade and moss, and flitted like a dream before the bewildered eyes of common folk.

Miss Nannie Yulee, daughter of Fernandina's distinguished citizen, David L. Yulee, starred as "Queen of Flowers." She was complimented on her "charming dignity" by the ecstatic correspondent who expressed hope that "next season's hotel guests might once more enjoy The Land of Flowers."

Skating parties, calico parties at which only calico was worn, poverty socials, and "backward" parties to which the girls invited the boys and called for them at their homes were only a few of the Lyceum-held social events described in the *Mirror*. Chinese lanterns appeared to be the favorite decorations. The *Mirror* reported the Lyceum's use by both black and white members of the community. In the issue dated December 13, 1879, there was an account of a bazaar and entertainment in the Lyceum by members of the "A.M.E. and Zion churches."

The builders of the Lyceum wisely envisioned multipurpose uses of the facility. Auditorium chairs were numbered to correspond with numbered storage bins, and were easily removed to make way for skating, dancing, or dining. Not only was the auditorium of the Lyceum used for entertainment from the stage and dance floor, it was also used for city and county court. For court sessions, unlike more genteel occasions, the floor was strewn with sawdust in anticipation of tobacco-chewing jurors and spectators.

Even after the Golden Age of Amelia Island had ended, the Lyceum remained a focal point for island entertainment and political gatherings. A ball, reported in the *Mirror* on March 2, 1911, was held to benefit the Cemetery Association. The guests arrived costumed as Colonial ladies and gentlemen. Patrick C. Kelly dressed as General George Washington; the mayor, Colonel N. B. Borden, led the Grand March with his wife Flossie who was dressed as Martha Washington. The *Mirror* noted that guests enjoyed dancing to the Grand March, Waltz, Quadrille Polka, Lancers, and the Virginia Reel. In 1905, the Lyceum opened a new era of local entertainment when it showed its first movie, featuring scenes of the Russo-Japanese War.

Update

The latter years of the Lyceum were noted in the *Fernandina News Leader* on February 2, 1952, when the Ritz Theater, as it had been renamed, was razed:

In 1917, the building was purchased by Jackson Mizell, and Walter S. Whitney was manager. In 1920, Mizell sold the building to Albert Hirth, who operated it under the name of Rex Theater. In 1934, D. B. White purchased the building and operated it as a typical movie house called the Ritz Theater where popcorn and soft drinks and cigarettes were sold, and movies were viewed through a haze of tobacco smoke. It was under White's ownership that sound movies were shown for the first time. C. E. Beach operated the Ritz until 1948, when he built the Ilan [sic] Theater, a Quonset-hut type building located on Atlantic Avenue, west of the city waterworks.

The last days of the Lyceum, occurring just as the era of television was beginning, marked the end of a long and colorful era of Amelia Island entertainment.

Blind Tom - Entertainer who appeared at Lyceum Hall.

The Newport of the South
Nassau Light Artillery and Fernandina Light Infantry

Several State of Florida militia organizations existed on Amelia Island during the Golden Age. Although the official purpose of these organizations was to maintain law and order in emergency situations, with emergency situations rarely occurring, the Fernandina organizations were in effect elite social clubs with memberships seemingly more interested in grand uniforms, "hops," banquets, and social functions than as serving as serious keepers of the peace. The two militia clubs whose activities were most prominently reported in the *Florida Mirror* were the Nassau Light Artillery and the Fernandina Light Infantry, both organized in 1879. Not to be outdone, "the colored men of Fernandina have organized a military company with Ed Hearn as Captain," reported the *Florida Mirror* on October 11, 1879. It is not known how long this military company survived or what activities it may have sponsored.

Notice of the organization of the first organized militia, the Nassau Light Artillery, appeared in the March 8, 1879, *Florida Mirror*: "Those wishing to become members of an artillery company now forming, please meet at the Lyceum." When making application for membership, satisfactory personal references were required. The April 26, 1879, *Florida Mirror* reported the organization complete. Forty men, "the

best in the city" were enrolled. They wore elegant uniforms
and displayed "two guns and side arms" furnished by Florida
Adjutant General J. J. Dickison, of Confederate fame. A letter
of congratulations and encouragement to the Nassau Light
Artillery from Dickison contained a promise to "order you
some sabers from Ordnance Department at Washington"
(*Florida Mirror*, May 3, 1879). The April 26, 1879, *Mirror*
listed officers of the organization, including D. E. Maxwell,
Captain; E. P. Noyes, First Lieutenant; G. N. Saussey, Second
Lieutenant, J. E. Wandell, Secretary and Treasurer; and T.
Starbuck, Surgeon.

Records of the Nassau Light Infantry include the
treasurer's report dated June 9, 1880—"cash from the ladies
$121.05 and a disbursal to Charles Angel for rent, $32.50"
and purchases of officers' cavalry swords. A subsequent
statement, dated July 27, 1880, included "1 Doz. Goblets,
$1.50." (The goblets presumably got more regular use than

Loyal Fernandina veterans of the Confederacy organized as
the Nassau Light Artillery Company .

AIMH

the cavalry swords.) Records show a total membership of 35, including 9 officers, 13 privates, 1 honorary member and 12 paying members. Correspondence shows that architect Robert V. Schuyler applied for membership on May 23, 1884.

A military ball at the Mansion House celebrated the Nassau Light Artillery's organization. The ball, according to the *Florida Mirror* of May 10, 1879, was a "grand success...44 couples on the floor at one time." An invitation to the ball in the files of the Amelia Island Museum of History "respectfully solicits your company at the Mansion House on May 7, 1879." According to the invitation, the reception and invitation committees would be wearing white rosettes and the floor manager, a rosette of red. The military "hops" at the Mansion House and the Lyceum must have been colorful occasions with the bright uniforms of the local militia mingled with the uniforms of the captains of ships from all over the world anchored in the harbor.

A hand-colored photograph of the Nassau Light Artillery, owned by the Amelia Island Museum of History, shows twelve men in handsome blue-gray uniforms trimmed in red. Pictured in the photograph are the twelve charter members of the company: D. E. Maxwell, general manager of the Florida Railroad; Dr. Theodore Starbuck, port physician; Mr. W. H. Garland, tax collector and property appraiser; W. O. Jeffreys, merchant and builder; G. W. Saussey; George Gilchrist; A. O. MacDonell, superintendent of the Florida Railroad; W. B. Thompson, state senator for seven years; Emil O. Friend, merchant; and, according to the donor, "two [unnamed] gentlemen from the north." The photograph confirms that the organization was "composed of middle aged business men of our city...." (*Florida Mirror*, Aug. 16, 1879).

The Nassau Light Artillery, equipped with a ceremonial banner made by their ladies and wearing handsome uniforms and side arms, attended celebrations to unveil a Confederate marker in Macon, Georgia, and a "Jasper Centennial" in Savannah (*Florida Mirror*, Oct. 18, 1879). They had monthly dress parades at the Lyceum. In the spring of 1880, the Nassau Light Artillery moved into the top floor of the Angel Building, at the northwest corner of Third Street and Centre: "They will have a pretty little hall....a pleasant place for social meetings" (*Florida Mirror,* May l, 1880).

The "pretty little hall" in the Angel building almost comes alive in the May 29, 1880, *Florida Mirror.* The reporter described the armory hall neatly decorated for an "Artillery Supper," called a "perfect success." "Guns were polished for the occasion and tastefully decorated and dressed with flowers and vines and looked truly harmless as munitions of war." Prior to the supper, G. Saussey, chairman of the committee in charge of the entertainment, on May 18, 1880, wrote a letter to the officers and members of the club. In the letter, Saussey reported that the plan of enlisting help from the ladies had been "sanguin [sic] of success. We have every reason to believe that the affair will prove pleasant and successful." The *Florida Mirror* of October 9, 1880, reported that the Nassau Light Artillery had organized a Rifle Club. The ladies would be allowed to shoot.

The gala celebration of the second anniversary of the Nassau Light Artillery was held at the Lyceum, and, according to the *Fernandina Express*, March 10, 1881, it was "the most *recherché* affair that has occurred in Fernandina since the war." "At four in the afternoon the company assembled at their armory in full uniform and proceeded to the common to engage in the prize drill. Mr. Louis Horsey was declared best-drilled soldier." That evening, at the gala anniversary celebration, "our own native wine of the finest flavor seems to add jest and humor to the toasts and impromptu speeches and songs." At dinner, toasts were made "To the Anniversary of the Nassau Light Artillery;" "To the Ladies....God Bless them;" "To the Press, the great organ of public opinion.... the motor of this country;" and "To our guests." At eleven o'clock the table was abandoned and those who desired tripped the light fantastic. Thirty-two couples danced 'til three o'clock, not bad for the "middle-aged businessmen."

At a more serious time, as a memorial to the slain President James A. Garfield, the *Fernandina Express* on October 1, 1881 reported that the Nassau Light Artillery fired a 21-gun salute at eleven o'clock and one gun every half hour throughout the day. The Light Artillery celebrated its third anniversary on March 11, 1882, with a banquet at the Lyceum.

A second militia group, the Fernandina Light Infantry, was organized at about the same time as the Nassau Light Artillery. The organization expressed its thanks "to the Ladies of Fernandina in helping us procure uniforms by entertainment and supper given in the Lyceum Hall on the 18th instant" (*Florida Mirror*, Mar. 1, 1879). On July 5, 1879, the *Mirror* reported that the Fernandina Light Infantry had paraded in full uniform for the Fourth of July celebration. Twenty-three of their membership competed at the state level against other militia groups and had won second prize (*Florida Mirror,* Feb. 22, 1879).

Membership of the Fernandina Light Infantry included James McGiffin, Lieutenant; T. B. Livingston, Lieutenant; J. D. Streety, Sergeant; J. W. Starke, Second Corporal; Henry Burns, Third Corporal; and Privates D. Alverson, James Mock, M. Ferreira, James McWaters, Rich Godfrey, John O'Donald., Wm. Godfrey, Walter Smith, Wm. Mangum, Henry Sneed, R. Manucy, Wm. Streety, and George Wood.

There is little doubt when reading an excerpt of a letter written by D. M. Hammond of Fernandina, and published in the *New York Tribune,* on August 31, 1880, that the politics of the day may have infiltrated the meetings and practices of the two militia organizations. Although evidence of illegal action by Fernandina's militias is missing from the pages of the *Florida Mirror,* similar militias throughout the South had gained notoriety for the violence and intimidation the exerted to maintain racial and social control. Hammond's letter expressed derision that the two organizations, "armed with United States arms.... have never "owned, used, or carried a [United States] flag.....There are cases where the members have cut away the plate marked 'U. S. A'. and have substituted some old symbol of their lost cause marked 'C.S.A.'...They allow some Northern men and foreigners to borrow the Custom-House flags to ornament the hall on festive occasions but nobody has yet seen a Southern man or woman touch one [United States flag] and they are careful that they shall be placed when they are used where Southern people are not compelled to walk under them." Lawyer D. M. Hammond labeled these accusations "straws in the wind." During the Civil War, Hammond had been superintendent in charge of contraband [escaped slaves] on Amelia Island.

Hammond's letter caused obvious chagrin in the ranks of both the Nassau Light Artillery and Fernandina Light Infantry. The two militia groups vented their ire in the September 18, 1880, edition of the *Florida Mirror.* Both organizations sent letters to make "public denial" of the allegations made by Hammond. The Fernandina Light Infantry denied that any substitution of emblems had been made, and that the Infantry did indeed use two United States flags in dress parades. James McGiffin, who signed the letter signified, "these are facts, not straws." The Artillery endorsed the Infantry letter and added, "General Grant's visit to Fernandina was the occasion of a public parade, the Artillery giving the General a national salute. By him [Grant] the absence of the flag was unnoticed...." J.H. Prescott and Thomas Kydd signed the letter for the Nassau Light Artillery.

On at least one occasion, one of the militia groups interrupted its social schedule to serve a military function. The *Florida Mirror* of July 9, 1881, reported that the Fernandina Light Infantry was called in to quell a disturbance attributed to a group excursion visiting from Jacksonville on the 4th of July. "Principals of both colors were put in jail...There was no further trouble." Subsequent news in the *Florida Mirror* concerning the Light Artillery and Light Infantry was scarce. The May 10, 1884, *Florida Mirror* reported, "The former companies Nassau Light Artillery and the Fernandina Light Infantry have reorganized as the Fernandina Volunteers with 29 members enrolled. "Rev. H. S. Yerger has been elected chaplain..." (*Florida Mirror*, May 31, 1884).

The Fernandina Volunteers received little subsequent notice in the *Mirror*. A small notice of yet another military group appeared in the *Florida Mirror* on August 28, 1894, the Island City Guards. All that is known of this group is found in the notice that eight members had left for an encampment in Palatka "with new and elegant uniforms." Apparently, the militia groups had lost their initial enthusiasm. Soon, however, conflicts with Spain over the island of Cuba allowed Fernandina gentlemen an actual taste of military life.

The 1800 Catharine Greene Miller four-story tabby mansion burned in 1866, photographed here before the Carnegie restoration of the 1880s.

JHJ

The Newport of the South
Cumberland Island and Dungeness

No account of Amelia Island's Golden Age can be complete without mention of her Georgia sister island across the river. Catharine Greene's imposing four-story Cumberland Island home Dungeness, later restored to glory by its Golden Age mistress Lucy Carnegie, played a significant and pleasant role in Amelia Island's Golden Age. Excursions to Cumberland Island were *de rigueur* for Amelia's residents, and especially for the tourists staying at the elegant Egmont Hotel. The haunting tabby ruins of Dungeness amid the beauty of the remote and wild island intrigued all visitors before the ruins were restored to life by the Carnegie family in 1885. On December 7, 1878, the *Florida Mirror* proclaimed: "During the winter an excursion or picnic to Dungeness is the great event of the season with our northern visitors to Fernandina. No one should visit Florida without spending a week or two at the Egmont, the best hotel in the South [and] visiting Dungeness....There is no place more sadly beautiful on the Atlantic Coast and around which there hangs such a halo of romance" (*Florida Mirror*, Mar. 1, 1879).

The "sadly beautiful" ruins which lured locals and visitors to Cumberland Island during the Golden Age were those of "Dungeness," a house built around 1800 by Catharine Greene Miller, widow of Revolutionary War hero Nathaneal

Greene. General Greene died on June 19, 1786, and ten years after his death, his widow married Phineas Miller, her plantation manager. It is said that Catharine Greene Miller's fine house stood on the site of a hunting lodge built by James Oglethorpe, founder of the Colony of Georgia, who named the lodge "Dungeness" to honor England's Earl of Cumberland whose country seat in Kent bore that name. Catharine died at Dungeness in 1814. Her grave marker in the nearby Greene-Miller cemetery contains the words: "In memory of Catharine Miller, Widow of the late Major General Nathaneal Greene, commander in chief of the American Army in the Southern Department in 1783."

At Catharine's death, her youngest daughter, Catharine Louisa Greene Shaw, inherited Dungeness. In turn, Louisa, as she was called, left it to her nephew, Phineas Miller Nightingale. According to the *Florida Mirror* of March 31, 1883, during the Nightingale ownership, a number of freed slaves were "either placed there [at Dungeness] or allowed there by the Freedmen's Bureau and by their carelessness or willfulness caused its destruction by fire" in 1866. Whatever the cause, Dungeness burned to a tabby shell and the "crumbling ruins were soon covered with creeping vines."

Confederate General William George MacKay Davis was named as the "recent purchaser" of Dungeness in the March 20, 1880, edition of the *Florida Mirror*. He bought the property from the Nightingales. When President Ulysses S. Grant visited Amelia Island in January of 1880, owner General Davis escorted Grant and his party on an excursion to the "baronial ruins" of Dungeness. In a less affable time, months after Appomattox, on December 25, 1865, the *New York Times* described "Brig. Gen. W. M.G. Davis" as a "lawyer notorious for his imperiousness said to have been the biggest tyrant in the Confederate army. He never received calls from officers unless fully attired and equipped." Notwithstanding the unflattering sketch of General Davis in the *New York Times*, the *Mirror* pictured Davis as a gracious host who welcomed visitors to his newly purchased Dungeness property. One visitor was George M. Barbour, who wrote glowingly of the scenic Dungeness site in *Florida for Tourists Invalids and Settlers,* published in 1882:

"I never tire of its loveliness. Such teeming gardens, such brilliant flowers, such wide fields, such noble groves of grand old live oaks and magnolias, such oysters, game and fish. Could I tire of Dungeness? Dreamy, romantic, delicious, entrancing Old Dungeness? No never!"

The lush island sustained highly successful fields and orchards. A particular interest of General Davis was the culture of olives, described in several notices in the *Florida Mirror.* One article mentioned that Davis had sent to France and Italy for information on establishing olive groves as oil producing crops (*Florida Mirror,* Jan. 21, 1880). According to Mary Bullard's *Cumberland Island: A History,* at the time of Thomas Carnegie's interest in purchasing General Davis's Cumberland Island property, Davis wrote to Carnegie that there were "several hundred orange trees" at Dungeness bearing fruit, and six hundred old olive trees....the yield is very great." "There are many quince, pear, peach, apricot, and plum trees." Davis also mentioned Japanese plums and grape vines. Statistics compiled in 1849 by the state of Georgia list banana plants, lemons, figs, pomegranates, melons, citron, olives, oranges, potatoes, and corn growing on the Dungeness acreage. Captain George T. Davis, Amelia Island historian, remembered that some of the original olive trees survived on Cumberland Island until killed by a severe freeze and that Lucy Carnegie harvested lumber from the trees to fashion a parquet floor and to panel an elevator and hall.

In addition to General Davis's obvious interest in olive and orange culture, he also attempted to improve the breed of the marsh tackies [wild ponies] found on Cumberland Island since the time of Oglethorpe. The following appeared in the *Florida Mirror* on February 19, 1881: "General Davis's purpose securing a number of marsh ponies from the Carolina Islands and placing them on Cumberland Island with view of raising and introducing the stock. The Carolina pony is far superior to the marsh tackies which are seen on this and adjacent islands, and we trust General Davis will be most successful." Mary Bullard mentions that the Carnegies, too, were interested in improving the breed of the wild Cumberland Island horses to the extent that they introduced mustangs from the west and even a horse from the imperial Russian stud farms.

General Davis's ownership of the Dungeness properties was short-lived. The *Mirror* reported on June 11, 1881: "We have learned that General Davis has sold Dungeness to parties from the North." The "parties from the North" were Lucy and Thomas Carnegie of Pittsburgh, Pennsylvania. Thomas was in business with his more famous brother, steel magnate Andrew Carnegie. Amelia Island's "new neighbor, Thomas Carnegie, is building a new mansion worthy of its glorious site," that of the ruins of Catharine Greene's Dungeness. "The mansion will be of architecturally commanding proportions, beautiful in detail, and is to be built of granite...a noble object on a noble landscape" (*Florida Mirror*, Apr. 1, 1882). The preparations for the groundbreaking for the "palatial mansion of Mr. Carnegie" were reported in the *Mirror* on November 10, 1883. On March 1, 1884, the *Mirror* described the Carnegie yacht *Missoe* "bedecked in bunting in honor of laying of the foundation for Dungeness." The contractors presented Mrs. Carnegie with a silver square, level, and trowel in honor of the ceremony. Sadly, Thomas died at age 43, before the house was completed.

With the building of the new Dungeness, visitors from Fernandina no longer had the freedom to wander the stately ruins of Catharine Greene's house, her orchards and gardens, or to enjoy the many other wonders of the island. Notices in the *Florida Mirror* discouraged any further picnics and excursions to Cumberland Island. (See *Florida Mirror,* Mar. 17, Mar. 29, May 17, 1884). Fernandina locals may have understood that boatloads of Fernandina's Sunday school classes and Egmont visitors posed a danger and nuisance at the construction site, but they also must have felt sadness as the romantic tabby walls and four tall chimneys of Catharine Greene's Dungeness gave way to the new and palatial Carnegie-built Dungeness.

The Carnegie Dungeness as it appeared in the 1880s. After the death of Thomas Carnegie, his widow, Lucy, expanded the mansion to better accommodate her children.

AIMH

Reporters from the *Florida Mirror* were invited to view the building at its completion in 1885 and they wrote enthusiastic articles about the magnificent structure. One has only to look at photographs of the gleaming new edifice, its gardens and accompanying structures, to comprehend the awesome effect they must have had on the reporters who gazed upon it. From its completion, the stately new Dungeness and the lavish homes of the Carnegie's children that soon surrounded it were the beloved summer homes of Lucy Carnegie and her large family. Through several generations, good times, bad times, joys and sorrows took place on their splendid Cumberland refuge.

Although uninvited visitors from Fernandina were now forbidden to travel to the Shangri-la across the river, Lucy Carnegie's steam yacht the *Missoe* made daily trips to Fernandina for supplies and mail to be distributed to Cumberland families. Worthy causes such as the Library Association and First Presbyterian Church occasionally benefited from Carnegie generosity. The Carnegie family is believed to have supported half the cost of a $2200 purchase of the pipe organ installed in the Presbyterian Church in 1905. Carnegie men from time to time found Fernandina's Palace Saloon a welcome refuge from Cumberland domesticity. For years to come, bonds of friendship and trade continued to enrich both island communities.

Update

A scattered family and changing times eventually brought an end to the halcyon years of the Carnegie family's Dungeness. By the 1930s, valuable paintings and furnishings had been removed. In the 1950s, the house was closed and most of the remaining furnishings dispersed. Although the Carnegie purchase and the building of a new Dungeness ended the pleasant and popular Golden Age excursions from Fernandina, poachers, as they had done for generations, continued to take an unlawful share of deer, turkeys, quail, wild hogs, turtle eggs, and oysters found in abundance on Cumberland Island. Like its predecessor, the Carnegie Dungeness succumbed to flames, apparently set by these intruders. On June 26, 1959, the *Florida Times Union* declared the sad news: "The 44 room mansion of the late Mr. and Mrs. Thomas Carnegie on nearby Cumberland, once a showplace and retreat of the rich, was destroyed by fire last night.

It is believed acrimonious poachers set the blaze." Locals, to this day, widely acknowledge that disgruntled poachers, did indeed, spitefully torch the beautiful mansion; some may know who struck the match. Far into the night of

On 24, 1959, the long abandoned Dungeness was set ablaze by unknown poachers angry over the family's island hunting restrictions.

AIMH

179

the burning, disconsolate locals, standing on the docks of Fernandina and St. Marys, watched the lurid red glow of the flames of a dying Dungeness. They grieved the loss as of a death in the family.

After years of complicated negotiations between property owners and the Department of the Interior, Cumberland Island, in 1975, was officially declared a National Seashore. Today's visitors to Greyfield Inn, and those taking a tour of the National Seashore, now look with awe upon the "sadly beautiful ruins" of Thomas and Lucy Carnegie's Dungeness—a relic of Cumberland Island's Golden Age.

Dungeness as it is today, in ruins, as it has been since the 1959.

JHJ

The Newport of the South

The Trolley

A delightful photograph, probably taken in 1909, depicts the joy of a trolley ride to "Amelia Beach," as the eastern terminus of the trolley's route leading from Fernandina's downtown was called. The picture shows three open-air trolley cars in tandem, loaded with happy school children most likely headed for a fine outing on the beach. The Golden Age was in decline when the photograph was taken, but clearly, the picture shows the pleasure of the trolley ride whatever the date. The trolley in the photograph was the last of several public conveyances that, for many years, transported residents and visitors from town to the beach.

Beginning in 1878, transportation from town to the beach was a cherished amenity when guests of the newly built Egmont Hotel, and probably local citizens as well, rode to the beach in special Florida Railroad cars which they boarded at the hotel's Seventh and Beech Street location. The route followed Beech Street toward the ocean.

The short journey to the beach by the less affluent resident population could be made on an oyster shell road that followed Centre Street east to the ocean. On this road, residents could easily walk, ride bicycles, or use their own horse-drawn conveyances to access the beach, but on January 29, 1881, a happy reporter for the Florida Mirror exclaimed: "How about our horsecars from the city to the beach!" This "daily omnibus" was established by McGinnis and Rawson, with teams furnished by Mr. Courter (*Florida Mirror*, Feb. 19, 1881, and May 21, 1881). The *Fernandina Express* noted on June 18, 1881, "The regular busline to the beach leaving the city at 6 o'clock in the evening seems well patronized, the vehicle is generally well filled."

The "busline," really a horse-drawn omnibus, was to give way several years later to a real beach railroad. The *Mirror*, on March 3, 1883, reported that the Florida legislature had passed a bill to incorporate the "Fernandina and Amelia Beach R.R. Company." The principals of the company named in the *Mirror* were W.N. Thompson, Samuel A. Swann, D.E. Maxwell, W.B.C. Duryee, and A.O. McDonell. A beach railroad, the applicants for corporation stated, "would supply a long-needed demand."

Although survey lines for the two mile beach railroad had been completed by 1883, construction of the road-

The horse drawn beach trolley of the 1880s.

Davis Family

bed, and the laying of rails and crossties was still going on in May, 1885. The road was broad gauge, laid with the same iron used by the Florida Railway and Navigation Company. The western terminus of the road began at the waterfront depot and the route ran south on First Street [also called Front Street] to Beech, which it followed toward the ocean. Excursion trains from Jacksonville and elsewhere could be switched to connect with the new beach line.

The *Florida Mirror* of June 13, 1885, reported "The Y on the beach end of the Fernandina and Sea Beach R.R. will be completed tonight. For the present, the road will use the passenger coaches of the Florida Railway and Navigation Company. The locomotive will be smoke-consuming, thus preventing all danger from flying sparks to the dwelling houses along the route, and insuring safety from the disagreeable smoke" (*Florida Mirror*, May 9, 1885). One month later, the *Mirror* reported, "The first passenger train over the Fernandina and Sea Beach Railroad was run last Saturday evening. It was a complimentary trip to our citizens and was well patronized" (*Florida Mirror*, Jun. 13, 1885). A schedule, believed to be for the original runs of the beach train, appeared in the June 20, 1885, issue of the *Florida Mirror*:

> Trains leave Fernandina for the beach
> Week-days at 6:30, 9:00, and 11:20 A.M.
> 2:55, 4:35, 7:10, and 8:30 P.M.
> Trains Leave the Beach for Fernandina
> At 6:45, 9:20, 11:40 A.M.
> 3:15, 5:00, 7:30, 10:30 P.M.

On August 29, 1885, the *Mirror* reported: "The Fernandina and Amelia Beach R.R. carried over 1000 passengers on the occasion of the excursion and ball at Amelia Beach Pavilion." The *Mirror*, on September 5, 1885, pronounced the railroad "a complete success, the patronage having reached the expectation of the proprietors of this enterprise."

Little is noted in the *Mirror* about the beach railroad after the excitement of its opening in 1885 faded with the train's accustomed use, but it may be presumed that it played an important role in the lives of Fernandina's citizens, and, in the gradual development of Amelia Beach. As the lure of Henry Flagler's more luxurious hotel attractions further south made Fernandina's charms less desirable, it is believed the Fernandina and Amelia Beach Railroad ceased running around 1900.

Amelia Island residents and loyal tourists, however, could not long do without public transportation to their beloved beach. The tracks of the abandoned railway were to come alive, once again, for yet another beach railway, this time an electric street railway. According to the *Florida Mirror* of July 2, 1898, the City Council was once more asked to take action on the application of a franchise for the trolley that the oldest citizens of Fernandina still remember with nostalgia and affection. "Messrs. Lukenbill, Sahlman, and Latham were appointed to investigate." Effingham Bailey and John W. Simmons were the principals in the enterprise. Captain George T. Davis, noted local historian, adds Louis Hirth and John McGiffin to the roster of principal owners. The *Fernandina News* on July 24, 1902, reported: "Work on the trolley line is being pushed ahead. The rails are expected Tuesday. The generator, wire, and engine are already here." The previous steam-driven train had run on tracks from First Street, south to Beech Street, and eastward to the beach. The new ownership of the electric trolley chose a more circuitous route from Centre Street north to Seventh, to Ash, to Eleventh, then to Thirteenth Street where it connected with the old Beech Street tracks. The indirect route through town was said to have been adopted at the mandate of owners Effingham Bailey and John W. Simmons who wished the trolley route to go past their own residences, as well as the many other attractive homes along that particular route. Photographs of the electric trolley show happy groups of out of town excursionists disembarking at the steps of the Casino from a three-car trolley.

T. Howard Kelly, local journalist and author, mentioned the trolley in an article entitled "Fair Fernandina" that was published in the *Fernandina News Record* on March 21, 1913: "We see street cars whizzing to and from city to the beach.... street cars are operated on three principal streets and between the city and the beach." Kelly's glowing remarks seem ironic in retrospect, for it is believed the trolleys stopped running soon after Kelly's published article. All was not lost, however. The city of Fernandina assumed ownership of the tottering trolley line and began an aggressive campaign to market

The last of the electric trolleys stopped along Centre Street for a photo opportunity. A crowd of visitors from Jacksonville are abroad.   AIMH

the splendid beach and newly rebuilt public pavilions. New wires were strung for the trolley and even newly refurbished cars were ordered. The following appeared in the *Fernandina News-Record* on Friday, May 28, 1915:

> The beach project is progressing nicely and everything indicates that operations will begin by the middle of June. The street railway is complete with the exception of the trolley wire and that is being erected as rapidly as possible. The cars arrived the first part of the week and the bathhouses are being pushed to completion in order that people may be enabled to go and come and indulge in surf bathing while the pavilions are yet being constructed. It is believed these features of the project will be ready for operation within the next ten days.

A month later the Fernandina News-Record, June 25, 1915, noted that the city fathers proudly announced:

> Amelia Beach will open under the ownership and control of the municipality of Fernandina....The only seaside resort in the United States owned by a municipality.... Everything Nice and New. Automobile races, motorcycle races, foot races, pyrotechnic display....Everybody is coming. . .Join the throngs. .. . You may motor over the best hard roads in the State which lead right up to the big pavilion or the Seaboard Airline Railway will bring you right up to the spot at rates which are cheaper than walking.

The days of the city-owned trolley, sadly, were numbered. Fernandina's steadily declining economy during World War I and a growing number of automobiles hastened the trolley's demise. Helen Gordon Litrico, in the Fall 1992 issue of *Amelia Now*, quoted minutes of the city commission from September 4, 1918, that marked its end: "The Street Railway and Beach Committee was empowered to dispose of all rail and equipment, trolley wire and bonds at best price offered." The beloved trolley was no more.

The Newport of the South

Amelia Beach

Golden Age citizens of Amelia Island enjoyed their beautiful island beach and recognized it as a premier tourist attraction. A traveler from Ohio in "From the Atlantic to the Gulf Coast, Fernandina, Florida, January 30, 1883," transcribed from the *Mirror* in research notes by Alice P. Youngblood, described his visit to the "splendid beach which forms a pleasant driveway for ten or twelve miles. The scene on reaching the beach was one of animation, excited crowds betting on their favorites, and the riders running the horses up and down the smooth sandy bed; but it turned out that there was more animation than racing and the spectators returned to the city, while we took the long route four miles being over the lovely beach which though of sand is very hard and as smooth as a floor."

A few years later, *Webb's Florida,* in 1885, enthusiastically wrote: "One of the principal attractions of Fernandina is its magnificent sea-beach, which is reached from the city by a pleasant drive of two miles along a smooth shell road. For about 20 miles, in an almost straight line, the beach presents a hard-beaten, smooth surface, making it one of the finest drives in America." Tourists and Fernandinians tired of sunny beach attractions could also find a shady respite in a drive on the nearby road to Fort Clinch, opened in 1879 "for the benefit and pleasure of our citizens and guests" (*Florida*

Mirror, Mar 15., 1879). The overgrown and abandoned fort must have made a suitably "romantic" impression for the visitors who, after the Carnegie family purchased Cumberland Island, were no longer able to make excursions there to enjoy the spell of the ruined Dungeness.

Development on the beach, however, lagged that of "New Fernandina." According to an editorial found in the *Florida Mirror,* on April 23, 1881, "There are no houses of any kind at the beach except some small bath-houses or shelters." The editorial touted the need for a livery stable to make regular passage by horse drawn carriage to the beach, for expansion of bathing shelters, and further, Fernandina "should build a street railway to the beach." The *Mirror* reported "with great pleasure" on May 14, 1881, "that a movement is on foot to erect a commodious house of entertainment at the beach.... We hope the company incorporated some years since for a street railroad to the beach will reorganize under their charter and put the road in operation."

Shortly afterwards, on May 21, 1881, the *Florida Mirror* reported that "McGinnis and Rawson have established a daily [horse-drawn] omnibus line on the beach, remaining one hour and returning, at a very moderate round-trip ticket." With regular and dependable round-trip transportation to the ocean, Amelia Beach entered its own Golden Age. The *Fernandina Express*, on May 21, 1881, reported, "The stockholders of the Beach Holding Company and Shell Road Company held a meeting at the office of Mr. S. A. Swann, [and] C. W. Yulee, W. B. C. Duryee, H. E. Dotterer, T. Kydd, and S. A. Swann were elected a board of directors. The object of the company will be to erect a hotel on the beach and repair and keep up the shell road leading from the city to the beach." A further purpose of the incorporation, as reported in the *Mirror* on June 11, 1881, was "to receive the right of maintaining and collecting toll on a road connecting the beach with the city of Fernandina." Additional stockholders named were J. H. McGinnis and William Rawson, who had established the omnibus line, Calvin B. Dibble, and Gustave Stark. Capital stock was noted as $10,000.

The Strathmore, as the corporation's new hotel was named, was designed by Robert Schuyler, noted architect of most of Fernandina's important Golden Age buildings. The contract was soon let for the erection of the beach hotel to be located "400 yards south of the shell road, immediately on the beach....the foundation will be washed by the waters of the Atlantic." The hotel was expected to be 260 feet in length. "A dining room will be in the center in the form of a Saint Andrew's cross or the letter X," large enough to accommodate "large excursions." North of the dining hall "will be the gentlemen's reading, sitting, and smoking room....Verandahs will extend entirely around the building." In short order, The Strathmore opened to the public on August 12, 1881, "with every available room taken." The Strathmore proprietor added additional cots, but according to

The Strathmore Hotel.

AIMH

the *Mirror,* "was unable to accommodate all" (*Florida Mirror,* Aug. 12, 1881). Tourism on Amelia Beach was off and running.

"The Strathmore presents a fine appearance," the *Fernandina Express* reported in September of the opening year. "Ah the delights of a surf bath and lingering over the fine bill of fare at the Strathmore." An editorial in the *Florida Mirror,* on April 22, 1882, stated, "We have been curious to know why our popular beach hotel was named the Strathmore." Interviewed on the subject by a *Mirror* reporter, W. B. C. Duryee, as agent for the trustees of the company gave the reporter a lengthy biographical sketch of Claude Bowes Lyon, Earl of Strathmore, offered minute details of the Strathmore coat of arms, but gave no reason at all why the hotel was named Strathmore.

Less than a month after the Strathmore opened, a September 3, 1881, letter to the editor of the *Florida Mirror* from architect Robert Schuyler pleaded "that rumors be denied that the Strathmore was injured by the late storm.... An examination during and after high tide found no injury, and no danger....as the sound of rolling water beneath the house is always disagreeable to and alarming to the nervous. We are now getting material on the ground to shut out the sea." The sea, however, was not to be stopped. The *Mirror* of September 1, 1883 reported the Strathmore "so near the water that at very high tide the breakers almost wash the front steps."

There is no doubt that the Strathmore Hotel spearheaded the development of the beach on Amelia Island. At the same time the Strathmore was under construction, Mr. A. Steil was building a beach restaurant that would be named the Atlantic Pavilion: "Mr. Steil's restaurant is nearly completed" noted the *Florida Mirror* on June 18, 1881. Mr. James McGiffin was the contractor. "Mr. Steil gave a free lunch to inaugurate the tastefully decorated building and announced that clam chowders will be served on Saturdays and Sundays throughout the season," also promising that "ice cream and lager will soon be in season by the sea." The next month, on July 2, 1881, the *Mirror* reported "Steil's restaurant under full headway....several bathrooms [sic] have been completed, bathing dresses provided. "The building was decorated with "picturesque flags and fluttering pennants."

Little is known of the Idle Hour, described as a "shore house" on Amelia Beach in *Webb's Historical Industrial and Biographical History of Florida.* The shore house "bearing the above euphonious title" was described as "constructed of wood, one and one-half stories in height, with a spacious piazza running completely around the buildings." The Idle Hour contained five sleeping rooms. Clam chowder and refreshments were served at all hours. Mrs. George Sweeny, widow of the Idle Hour's founder, was the proprietress. She promised to have "choicest oysters, fish etc. constantly on hand" (*Florida Mirror*, April 26, 1884). The Idle Hour, constructed in 1881, was located near the terminus of the Centre Street shell road.

A pavilion "erected by townspeople" in 1883 stood near the Strathmore. The *Florida Mirror*, on July 14, 1883 observed: "The pretty Pavilion and neat bathing houses on the beach attract much attention and deserve admiration." The *Mirror*, on July 21, 1883, called the Pavilion a "step in the right direction." According to the *Mirror* of September 1, 1883, the Pavilion contained thirty bathing closets and a large central room for picnics, skating, and dancing. It is likely that a storm damaged this structure. An editorial query appeared in the *Mirror*, on May 9, 1885: "Is not the pavilion to be rebuilt?" The query was happily answered in the *Mirror* on July 11, 1885: "A large pavilion for the benefit of the public

AIMH

A trolley has arrived at the Casino.

is being erected by the Fernandina Amelia Beach Railroad Company on Amelia Beach."

With easy transportation and other amenities in place, prosperous Fernandina citizens began to build summer homes to take advantage of the cool Atlantic breezes. According to notations in the *Mirror*, W. B. C. Duryee and several other residents built beach cottages in 1882. The H. J. Baker family was one of the first of the local families to move to the beach for the summer months, and the *Florida Mirror* of June 23, 1883, reported that Samuel Swann had erected, "for his private use, a row of bath houses and a platform for picnic parties." Mr. W. O. Jeffreys moved his family to the Atlantic Pavilion for the summer of 1884. To a reader of the *Florida Mirror*, it is evident that the townspeople delighted in beach activities.

Sadly, most of the Island's first beach structures lasted only a brief time. On October 2, 1898, most of Amelia Beach's buildings were swept away by hurricane winds and tides. Of the homes and businesses on the beach, only the Duryee cottage and a battered section of the proud Strathmore remained after the storm.

What was left of the Strathmore was used for a time as a beach pavilion or casino, one of the various casinos that Fernandina residents enjoyed for many years. Although contemporary casinos are usually associated with gambling, Golden Age casinos, like pavilions, were simply buildings used as public gathering places. In an old photograph, the name "Casino" appears on a banner flying from the staff of one of the towers of the Strathmore, while a later photograph shows it ruined after a fire.

The *Fernandina Record*, in June 1907, described another beach pavilion built by the Fernandina Amelia Beach Railroad Company some years after the Strathmore casino was destroyed. There were "facilities at different locations for the pleasure of both white and colored people." A large skating rink and bowling alley afforded "pleasure for not only the people of Fernandina, but to those who are learning that this is the most delightful beach in the State for the summer sojourn." A fine large building labeled "Casino" appears in a photograph, dated 1908, in the personal scrapbook of Elizabeth Swann Carroll, daughter of Samuel A. Swann, early promoter of Amelia Island. This building, the last one built by the railroad, also burned shortly after Miss Swann's photograph was taken.

After this brief hiatus, the popular beach casinos continued to be places of pleasure and delight to generations of beach enthusiasts of Amelia Island. In 1915, a third pavilion was built, this time by the city of Fernandina. The *Fernandina News Record,* on July 9, 1915, reported: "The new pavilion will be ready for dancing." The new pavilion was built on the site of the previous Casino, the northeast corner of what is now Atlantic Avenue and North Fletcher Avenue. Old photographs show beach visitors arriving at the 1915 Casino aboard the Fernandina trolley which stopped at the very steps of the building. The *News-Record* declared: "Amelia Beach will be officially opened for the season. July 15th is expected to be the biggest day in the history of Fernandina....Prizes will be given for the best dancing of the afternoon and evening." On June 25, 1915, it further bragged: "Amelia Beach will open under ownership and control of the municipality of Fernandina. The only seaside resort in the U. S. owned by a municipality!" On July 30, the *News-Record* invited the public: "Join the throngs! You may motor over the best hard roads in the state which lead right up to the big pavilion, or the Seaboard Airline Railway will bring you right to the spot at rates which are cheaper than walking!"

The casino built in 1915 was later moved across the street to be closer to the beach. A postcard of this pavilion noted that both Georgia and Florida visitors came to the Casino "in search of cool breezes." Older citizens of the island remember wide porches that could be shuttered against northeast winds and rows of rocking chairs and benches. The large open-air expanse was ideal for dancing—sometimes with out-of-town orchestras, sometimes with the local combo, and in the 1930s, with a jukebox. Local young people learned to dance in the Casino while their mamas rocked and gossiped in the comfortable chairs on the porch. They skated and bowled in that large, breezy, wonderful building. A bath house was downstairs. In winter, the dance floor turned into a basketball court where high-school teams practiced, and. before a loyal hometown audience, resolutely tried to best Maclenny, Hilliard, or Callahan.

A long list of lease-holders managed the city-owned Casino over the years. John J. Klarer and Townsend Weimer are remembered from the twenties; Herbert Buie, the Ferreira brothers, and Thomas Askins, from the thirties; and, in the last years of the Casino's existence, from 1939 to1946, Mom and Pop Hutchins ran the best restaurant in town before they built and moved on to the Seaside Inn.

Three Ferreira brothers, in a much simpler era than the present, submitted one summer a bid of $30 to run the casino for the season. Because no one else bid, they and their mother moved out lock, stock, and barrel to the living quarters of the casino to spend "the most wonderful summer of our lives" as custodians and managers of the place. At night, the musical Ferreira family played for the dancers, Ted and Vennie on the sax, and Louis and their talented mother at the piano.

Update

By the mid 1950s, the Casino was gone, replaced by a skating rink and restaurant, but the Buccaneer Trail, opened November 1950, had begun to revive the beach front community. In 1957, the Florida Legislature authorized the consolidation of Fernandina and Fernandina Beach. Although some still cling to the simple elegance of the name "Fernandina," Fernandina Beach was the aspiring resort community's name of choice.

Wars and Alarums
Yellow Fever

Yellow fever, sometimes called yellow Jack or yellow John, was a dreaded scourge on Amelia Island and other southern coastal areas where marshes abound. This disease, fortunately almost unknown in the United States today, got its name because of the jaundiced skin tones that signaled liver failure, the fatal signature of the worst infections. Alice Youngblood in *Seeing Fernandina* describes the terror of Fernandina's first known epidemic: "In 1818, a yellow fever epidemic broke out which was so devastating that even the United States Marines left the island. The town [Old Town] was almost depopulated, and many years passed before people returned in appreciable numbers to live there." Cases of yellow fever occurred each year, many of them quite mild, but serious epidemics marked by high death rates and wide-spread panic returned periodically with tragic results.

A story indicating the terror that yellow fever evoked in the Golden Age years is found in a privately owned document dated June 9, 1873, signed by pilots James Bell and J. H. Newton. In this document, the pilots vividly described a perilous incident that occurred during a season of yellow fever. In the midst of a rising storm, they spied the Norwegian bark *Anna* flying a distress signal as she sailed into Amelia Island waters bearing a cargo of sugar and molasses out of Havana, Cuba. When the pilots boarded the *Anna,* they found the captain, the mate, and five seamen dead, one dying, and two others sick of the fearsome disease. The *Anna*'s sick and dying crewmen were no longer capable of turning the ship into the winds of the dangerous storm. Pilots Bell and Newton hailed Captain Lewis A. Davis, who was standing by on the *James Guy*, to assist in turning the bark into the winds. Captain Davis agreed, but his crew refused to board the disease-ridden vessel. In spite of the threats of disease and hazardous winds, Captain Davis and the pilots Bell and Newton heroically risked their lives to save the distressed ship and those aboard.

Unfortunately, just as Fernandina was moving toward the greatest prosperity the community had ever known, an unusually severe epidemic outbreak of the fever struck in 1877. The first victim, a sailor on a Norwegian ship the *Bjorn,* succumbed in August. The press and leading businessmen, fearful of the fever's effect on the island's booming economy, at first tried to squelch the rumor that yellow fever was in the area, but the truth could not be suppressed.

Health officials quarantined the area, requiring travelers to produce passes upon entering or leaving Fernandina to show that neither they nor their close relatives had been in contact with any victim of the disease. Mail was perforated and placed on wire trays over burning sulfur to drive out the contamination, then thought by many to be spread by inorganic particles called "fomites." Other theories of the disease pointed to unhealthy vapors in the air, so cannons were brought from Fort Clinch and fired up and down the streets on the theory that the concussion would disrupt the vapors and kill the disease. Residents burned sulfur and tar to stave off infections. Houses where fever victims lived were fumigated and their clothes and bedding were destroyed. Residue from a local creosote company was trickled from barrels up one street and down the other in the hope that the strong odor permeating the air would somehow bring down the cause of the mystifying disease. Jacksonville declared a state of quarantine and placed guards around the city limits to keep out travelers from Fernandina (*Jacksonville Journal*, Dec. 12, 1975).

When the first rumor spread through Fernandina that yellow fever had appeared, some citizens hurried aboard one of the many passenger steamers in port and left town for what they believed to be safer places. Others went into the woods and built shelters, some retreating to shacks on Tiger Island across the river from Old Town. In a few cases, the terrifying disease caused such panic that victims of the fever were completely abandoned and left to die. Entire households were stricken, leaving none to care for those who were ill. In the epidemic of 1877, 1612 of Fernandina's citizens fell ill out of a population of approximately three thousand. There were ninety-five deaths (*Journal of the Florida Medical Association*, Apr. 1986).

In sympathy, Tallahassee's *Weekly Floridian* carried the following sad poetic lines on October 16, 1877:

Fernandina
Thou stricken city!
None may know
The weight of misery and woe now crushing thee.
Along thy streets with muffled tread
Tired undertakers with their dead
Move hurriedly
The awful pestilence is here
Like yellow autumn leaves and sere
The victims fall.
Both high and low, both young and old
The good, the beautiful, the bold
Are going—all!

There were many long remembered heroes and heroines of the yellow fever epidemics on Amelia Island. Dr. Theodore Starbuck, a physician from Savannah, moved to Fernandina to aid the devastated town. The Sisters of St. Joseph became beloved heroines of the community as they worked night and day to care for the sick and abandoned. All but two of the small group of nuns contracted the fever, and two of them, including the convent's Mother Superior, died.

At the height of the epidemic, Doctor Francis Preston Wellford, at that time president of the Florida Medical Association, and Doctor James Carmichael Herndon left their practices in Jacksonville and came to Fernandina to volunteer their professional help. Tragically, both succumbed, several days apart, to the virulent disease. U. Sinclair Bird, writing in the *Jacksonville Sun and Press,* described the obsequies of Dr. Wellford that took place in St. Peter's Church before his burial in the church's cemetery (October 12, 1877). Dr. Wellford's obituary reveals the weary desolation and sorrow of the stricken town:

The service was the most solemn and impressive I have ever attended. There were not six persons in the church who had not felt the touch of the pestilence. The clergyman [Owen P. Thackara] was pale and feeble from a recent attack-so weak that his voice now and then dipped and quivered. The organist and singers had been at death's door. The bearers, with the exception of a single one, had been down. The congregation was composed of convalescents, many who were pale and sallow and scarcely able to walk.... The sun was just setting while the clergyman said 'earth to earth, dust to dust, ashes to ashes.' The coffin was laid in the grave and loving hands laid the flowers on the stranger's grave, and with saddened hearts we returned to the chambers of sickness, to our desolated houses, and to our work of love.

In March 1879, Dr. Wellford's remains were removed from St. Peter's cemetery for reburial at his home in Fredericksburg, Virginia: "Citizens accompanied the remains to the steamer. Stores were closed...all the church bells and the fire bell tolled and the flag at the customs house was at half-mast...Thus was the last visible tie forever severed that bound the citizens of Fernandina to the man who gave his life that they might live" (*Florida Mirror*, Mar. 1, 1879).

Dr. Herndon was also buried in St. Peter's cemetery. His body was later removed to Savannah for re-burial in his family's plot in Bonaventure Cemetery, where his tombstone reads, "He finished a career of constant fidelity and Christian fortitude and professional devotion at Fernandina, Florida, answering there with his life the appeals of a stricken community and falling a lamented victim of the pestilence which desolated that city in the year 1877."

Although their graves were relocated, Dr. Wellford and Dr. Herndon are still memorialized in a stained glass window in the sanctuary of St. Peter's Episcopal Church. The Reverend Owen P. Thackara, rector of St. Peter's, in years to come would eulogize their memories near the anniversary of the doctors' deaths. On one such occasion, Dr. J. Baxter Upman, a regular winter visitor in the congregation, was so deeply moved by Thackara's tribute to the sacrificial death of the young doctors that he commissioned the window.

Another local hero of the epidemic was Dr. J. Denham Palmer, a prominent Fernandina physician. Although he had at first attempted to quiet the rumors that yellow fever was spreading in the booming town of New Fernandina, he is revered for his later distinguished service to the victims of the fever. In the *Florida Mirror* of March 1, 1879, he was affectionately called "old two baskets" for his habit of carrying two baskets as he made calls on suffering patients. In one basket he brought medicine, and in the other, nourishment such as condensed milk or beef bouillon. Dr. Palmer later served as an officer of the National Board of Health along the Gulf from Pensacola to New Orleans and up to Memphis. For his outstanding service to victims of a yellow fever epidemic in Nashville, the Howard Relief Association, an emergency aid organization that preceded the Red Cross, presented Dr. Palmer with a gold medal (*Florida Mirror,* Mar. 1, 1879).

Each summer brought its regular wave of illness, and authorities, with true dedication, faithfully carried out the preventative measures of the day. In a more enlightened age, the "fomites" and "vapors" that were accepted as causes of yellow fever in 1877 now appear to be ridiculous.

In 1881, however, Cuban scientist Carlos J. Finley concluded that the *Aedes aegypti* mosquito was the carrier of yellow fever. If indeed Fernandina's port masters and members of the City Council were aware of Finley's then unproven theory, it had no effect on their line of attack to control the fearsome disease. Local papers from 1877, when the worst epidemic occurred, until the 1890s reveal a relentless effort by authorities of the city and port of Fernandina to control the spread of the dreaded fever by any means, including the quarantine of vessels that entered Amelia Island waters from the hot, humid unsanitary ports of Cuba, the Caribbean islands, and South America. An editorial on February 8, 1879, in the *Florida Mirror* suggested that Havana, Cuba, might be the "hotbed" of the terrible scourge of yellow fever: "The way to deal with yellow fever is to attack it where it originates." Fernandina's port was therefore closed for three months to all vessels arriving from Cuba and South American ports (*Florida Mirror,* Apr. 19, 1878).

City Council members argued about the effects of quarantine and the Council struggled with decisions of economic losses versus fears that a vessel might carry more than cargo. An "ordinance" appeared in the *Mirror* of September 27, 1879: "Ships that arrive from infected ports shall not be permitted to leave quarantine or approach the city until after the occurrence of frost." Thomas Kydd, President of Council, and Norman Brownson, Mayor and Chairman of the Board of Health signed the ordinance. The ordinance, however, was repealed a month later (*Florida Mirror,* November 15, 1879). In spite of a perverse economic impact, stringent precautionary measures dictated by the port authorities continued. The holds of incoming vessels to Fernandina had to be fumigated with burning sulfur and tar, thought to kill the "fomites" or disrupt the unhealthy air perceived as sources of the fever. In addition to a period of quarantine at the station at Tiger Island and before taking on their cargo at the local docks, incoming ships were also required to jettison their ballast. Quantities of ballast may still be seen on Tiger Island and at various sites along the Amelia River (*Jacksonville Journal,* July 28, 1977).

Captain Frederick A. Small, of the schooner *Anita,* objected strongly to Fernandina's quarantine regulations in a letter to the editor of the *Mirror,* published on February 10, 1883. He complained that after leaving Martinique with a "clean bill of health," he found that in Fernandina's port his ship had to be fumigated. Captain Small grumbled that he had to hire a rowboat to bring a doctor aboard to perform the required services. Upon coming aboard, "when he [the port doctor] was good and ready, he goes down in the lower hold, puts a few sticks of pitch pine on top of my ballast, sets these sticks on fire, pours on some sulfur, and re-ascending to the upper decks coolly demands $25 for his arduous labors." The disgruntled Captain Small advised all masters of vessels bound for ports on the Saint Marys River to anchor at the Saint Marys Custom House rather than Fernandina:. "Extortion does not exist at St. Marys and besides you save $1 per foot on bar pillage."

In 1883, due to an epidemic in Pensacola, the upholstered railroad and sleeping cars of trains coming from west of the Chattahooche River were not allowed to enter the limits of Nassau County lest they harbor fever-inducing particles. The citizens of Fernandina, however, expressed their sympathy for victims of the Pensacola epidemic by organizing benefit baseball games and amateur talent programs at the Lyceum. The *Florida Mirror*, on September 23, 1883, published a revealing list of donors to the Pensacola Relief Fund:

Parties from the North	$35.00
E. P. Noyes	$1.00
Thos. Kydd	$2.00
John Barr	$1.00
George Fairbanks	$5.00
First Colored Baptist Church	$10.68
Little Charles Roux	$0.50

Yellow fever was not the only fearful scourge that marred the well being of the Golden Age. Malaria, also mosquito-born, was a chronic disease causing intermittent chills and fevers for many coastal residents. In 1883, city officials of Fernandina became anxious over an outbreak of smallpox that had occurred in Jacksonville. Passengers and their baggage from the infected city were quarantined, and only vaccinated passengers were allowed to disembark in Fernandina. The city commissioned George E. Wolff, assisted by four sanitary workers, to take a census of citizens who had been vaccinated against the disease. Wolff recorded that 1039 families were visited and 563 families were found to be vaccinated. The city physician was ordered to visit every unvaccinated inhabitant, and persons refusing the procedure "shall not leave their premises" (*Florida Mirror*, June 16, 1883).

Five years after the smallpox scare, another severe epidemic of yellow fever believed to have originated in Cuba spread to Key West, Tampa, and then Jacksonville, striking Amelia Island on September 17, 1888. Margaret Fairlie, in the *Florida Historical Quarterly*, October 1957, wrote of the fears engendered by this epidemic in Jacksonville and the surrounding area. Authorities set up a detention camp, Camp Perry, at Boulogne along the railroad tracks on the Florida side of the Saint Marys River. Railroad passengers from yellow fever stricken areas were detained and quarantined in the camp for ten days. Catherine Cope, in an article published in the *Charlton County Herald* on February 7, 1973, called conditions at Camp Perry "deplorable, with dilapidated tents, not enough bedding and little food. Everyone had to struggle to secure a bite to eat, and some said they would rather take the chance of getting the fever than to encounter worse things at the camp on the banks of the Saint Marys River." In spite of the quarantine, the Georgia town of Waycross would not allow refugees from infected areas to pass through town "even in locked [railroad] cars running at high speed."

Fairlie described a typical regimen of treatment that was recommended by the Jacksonville Auxiliary Sanitary Association in its *Report 138*:

> Give a hot mustard footbath with the patient in a chair under a blanket for fifteen minutes. After drying under the blanket place the patient in bed with hot

water bottles. Give five grains of calomel to adults and one-half this amount to a child. After three or four hours give a dose of castor oil or salts, also warm drinks of orange leaf tea. After the medicine acts, give one-half teaspoonful of nitre in cool water every two hours, and an enema if necessary. Give three tablespoonsful of beef or chicken broth or gruel and discourage vomiting.

In spite of such rigorous courses of treatment, there was little that nineteenth century medicine could do to combat yellow fever's high temperatures and liver failure effectively. A letter owned by Florence Roux Partin, dated October l, 1888, reveals the fear and stress experienced by residents of Fernandina during the epidemic. Florence Roux Partin's great grandmother wrote to her daughter from her home in Fernandina:

> Since I wrote you, there has been six funerals a day and it seems half the town is sick....The New York steamer was at the dock just crowded- [with passengers fleeing the epidemic] could not take on another one.... One shuts the house all up at four o'clock and [we] don't show our heads out after dark...sleep with shutters closed-night air is poison. I have sulphur and [illegible] on the stove....We all have to trust in the Lord. With lots of love to all.

Lucille Gallagher, in a poignant little story published in the 1930' in her class paper the *Sixth Grade Flashlight,* wrote of the grave of one of the Gainesville militiamen who died of yellow fever while serving in Fernandina during the longshoremen's strike that occurred just before the epidemic reached its peak. The young man was to be married in September but the summer's scourge of yellow fever struck him down. Miss Gallagher describes the tribute of his grieving sweetheart, who erected a marble shaft over his grave in Bosque Bello Cemetery and enclosed it with an iron fence that still may be seen today.

By the time an October frost ended the yellow fever epidemic, hundreds of Fernandinians had been stricken and fifty-two had died. George E. Wolff, sanitary inspector for the city of Fernandina, investigated every case. His careful reports furnished important data to governmental researchers in their study of the cause and eradication of the disease. His records contributed substantially to the government's final victory over one of the South's most virulent diseases.

Florida's experiences with yellow fever led to the formation of the State Board of Health in 1889 and the promulgation

Frank Leslie's Illustrated Magazine
Florida Memory Project

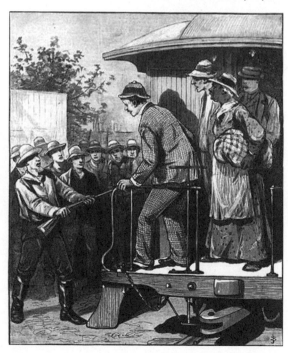

Unwanted and possibly infected train travelers being turned back.

of regulations concerning maritime quarantine that, in 1893, became the basis of U.S. Quarantine Board Rules and Regulations. Procedures required fumigation of ships, flushing of bilges, and observation for five days following treatment. Carlos J. Finlay's conjecture, made in 1881, that the *Aedes aegypti* mosquito was the carrier of yellow fever was not conclusively proved until after Walter Reed carried out successful experiments in 1900. Subsequently, massive efforts to control the *Aedes aegyptii* mosquito have ensured that yellow fever is virtually unknown in North America. No longer breeding death, Amelia Island's marshes are now treasured for their evocation of timeless beauty and serenity.

Wars and Alarums

The Filibustering Years

N
ot all of Fernandina's prosperity during her Golden Age came from the business pursuits of law-abiding citizens. For several years before the outbreak of the Spanish American War in 1898, many citizens of Florida responded with enthusiasm, and sometimes with flagrantly unlawful activities, to Cuban patriots seeking to wrest Cuba from Spanish rule. Floridians undoubtedly felt genuine concern for the oppressed Cubans, many of them working in cigar factories in Key West, Tampa, Fernandina, and elsewhere, but the temptations of immense profits from arms smuggling were also irresistible. Fernandina seamen were notorious for smuggling goods and slaves across the Georgia border before Florida became a U. S. territory, and they had recently polished their unofficial skills as blockade runners during the Civil War. With Fernandina's long record of governmental defiance, "filibustering," in this case illegally smuggling insurrectionists and arms to Cuba, was a natural progression.

The proximity of the east coast of Florida to Cuba gave Fernandina a ringside seat when Cuban insurrectionists in 1895 began in earnest to free their country from Spain. Led by the famous Cuban patriot José Marti, Cuban rebels plotted for years to free their country from the hated Spanish rule. Marti made his headquarters in New York City from 1881 to 1895, traveling frequently to Cuban cigar-making communities in Florida to rally support for the freedom fighters in Cuba and raise money to buy arms for an outright war of independence. In 1893, José Marti visited Fernandina and stayed for a week at the Florida House to make final preparations for the Cuban Revolutionary Party to transport Cuban sympathizers and supplies to Cuba from prearranged sites in Florida, Costa Rica, and Santa Domingo. While at the Florida House, Marti drew prominent businessman Nathaniel Barnett Borden, a prosperous factor for lumber and naval stores producers of the area and Fernandina's vice consul for Spain, into the conspiracy. With Borden's assistance, Marti engaged three yachts in New York and Boston, the *Amadis*, the *Lagonda*, and the *Baracoa*, as part of his elaborate plans. The three ships, allegedly headed for Central America, were to carry sympathizers and weapons disguised as agricultural workers and their tools. Once safely at sea, the vessels were to change course and deliver their illegal cargoes to Cuba.

The plot was set to unfold in the middle of January 1895. Unfortunately for Marti, the careful and costly arrangements he had made for the "Fernandina plan" went awry. Editors from Joseph Pulitzer's newspaper the *World* contacted their Fernandina correspondent T. A. Hall on January 7, 1895, to inquire about rumors regarding the *Amadis* and the *Lagonda*. Unfortunately for the Cuban cause, Hall served as a county judge as well as a *World* stringer, and he immediately contacted Fernandina's Collector of Customs George L. Baltzell. Marti's careful plans were exposed. The United States government detained the *Amadis* and the *Baracoa* at other ports and impounded the *Lagonda* when it arrived in Fernandina. Rather than being caught red-handed with his load of Cuban arms, the *Lagonda's* captain shortly before capture jettisoned his cargo of banana knives and rifles into the murky waters of Fernandina's harbor. Other armaments awaited in Borden's warehouse.

This story relating to Colonel Borden's filibustering activities appeared in the *New York Herald* on January 15, 1895. The breathless article read:

ARMS CONSIGNED TO MR. BORDEN CAME BY A MALLORY SHIP
One hundred and Fifty Cases of War Munitions Were Contained to the Original Shipment
SEIZED THE WHOLE LOT

"There was a decided sensation in this city tonight, when it was known that Collector Baltzell had seized a large number of cases....consigned to N. B. Borden about two weeks ago. There are about 130 of them and they were found in Borden's warehouse on the river front." Mr. Borden frankly confessed that they were there when the Collector approached him on the subject in his official capacity. The *New York Herald* story reported: One hundred and Fifty cases of War Munitions were Contained to the Original Shipment.... Broker Borden was just as chipper as ever this morning. He isn't worrying any and his brother Tom who is his partner, is said to have remarked since the seizure of the yacht: 'Oh well, we've got our money. We are all right.....' There is a report current here tonight that in dragging the harbor this afternoon near the *Lagonda* three cases of rifles were brought up from the bottom but nothing definite can be learned about it tonight."

Incredibly, the insouciant Borden went to court to sue the authorities for confiscating the supplies from his warehouse without proof that the merchandise was contraband. Although he won his case, he understandably lost his Vice Consulate and was replaced by Santiago Carrio, a Fernandina cigar manufacturer and Cuban by birth. The failure of Marti's

"Fernandina Plan," however, served to energize rather than discourage the Cuban freedom fighters.

Between Marti's setback and the official declaration of war against Spain in 1898, some of Fernandina's most prominent citizens joined Borden in the illegal opportunity to sell and deliver arms and supplies to Cuban rebels. Profits of $10,000 or more for expeditions regardless of their success were irresistible for local boat owners and Fernandina's waterfront became a place of intrigue. Maintaining official neutrality was the difficult, if not impossible, role of federal authorities in the port of Fernandina. United States gunboats patrolled the coast and all shipping activities were monitored. Notwithstanding the risks, local Cuban sympathizers were full of zeal, hungry for the fast buck, and fearless. A boatload of guns brought far more revenue than a boatload of mullet.

Florida filibustering activities became so aggressive that Spain hired Pinkerton detectives to uncover scheduled

N.B. Borden's Fernandina warehouse.

runs of arms to Cuba. Although American authorities were vested with the same obligation, they often turned blind eyes in sympathy for "Cuba libre." In spite of long odds, Fernandina's skilled captains and their vessels, loaded with men, guns and supplies, were repeatedly able to slip out past the gunboats guarding the harbor. *Seeing Fernandina* describes one such occasion. The *Paul Jones,* loaded with Cuban arms, was signaled by the U. S. gunboat *Vesuvius* to "come alongside." The *Paul Jones* responded, "'Too rough to come alongside." "Keep circling until the seas are calmer," ordered the *Vesuvius.* Obeying federal orders, the *Paul Jones* circled and circled in ever-widening circles until she disappeared into the darkness.

According to Alice Youngblood's research notes for *Seeing Fernandina,* Spanish Vice Consul Santiago Carrio was kept in a constant state of anxiety as Cuban sympathizers and local opportunists played hide and seek with authorities on Fernandina's waterfront. Cuban émigrés were said to hide around the docks during the day to scramble out of hiding at night to jump aboard vessels bound for Cuba, and telegraph wires were mysteriously cut or redirected between Jacksonville and Fernandina. The vessels the *Three Friends,* the *Dauntless,* and the *Commodore* became particularly famous for their flagrant and lucrative filibustering commissions. These vessels were common sights in Fernandina waters.

The *Three Friends* was most notorious. She was named for three friends who owned her, the brothers Napoleon and Montcalm Broward and George DeCottes, a Jacksonville businessman. The *Three Friends* was a tugboat built for salvage, or "wrecking" as it was then called, and towing. Tugboats had a special advantage, because they could claim to be searching for a supposedly wrecked ship if questioned by suspicious authorities, a claim difficult to challenge in court. Unlike most tugs, the *Three Friends* was also built for speed, a quality that served her captain and crew well during their unofficial ventures. The *Three Friends* made at least half dozen trips to Cuba. On her first filibustering mission, she was loaded with "100 tons of coal, 60 barrels of water, two cannon, 500 pounds of dynamite, 3000 Winchester rifles, 500 machetes, 1 million priming caps, 500 pounds of sulfur, and Cuban leader General Enrique Colasso. All but the General were labeled 'groceries'" (*Florida Times Union,* Nov. 7, 1993).

Florida's filibustering is the stuff of which movies are made. Fernandina's Collector of Customs George L. Baltzell, whose duty it was to clear all vessels coming in and going out of the harbor, was said to enjoy a game of poker. At a time when the legendary *Three Friends* had been impounded for gunrunning, owner Napoleon Broward was determined not to let a small thing like the loss of his vessel stop the flow of guns to Cuban freedom fighters. With blatant disregard of the impoundment papers posted on his vessel, Broward surreptitiously loaded the *Three Friends* with "tomatoes and other groceries" ready for delivery to Cuba and then commenced to engage Collector of Customs Baltzell in an intense poker game.

Far into the night the game went on. When the rapt attention of all parties was on the "cards and chips," the *Three Friends* cast off her lines with "Dynamite" Johnny O'Brien at the helm and slipped out of Fernandina's port, loaded not with "tomatoes and other groceries," but with nitroglycerine, cases of rifles, and Cuban émigrés from the cigar factories of Florida. Ralph D. Paine, a young newspaper reporter, secretly came aboard to join the émigrés. His boss William Randolph Hearst was using every opportunity to exploit if not to foment the news relating to the fight for Cuban independence, and, as a publicity stunt, Hearst commissioned Paine to carry a gold and jewel encrusted sword to the legendary Cuban General Maximo Gomez.

The *Three Friends*, bound out of Fernandina after the spellbinding poker game, entered Cuban waters and prepared to unload her contraband. She was discovered in the act by the Spaniards, but made a hair-raising escape under fire. It was too dangerous to unload on Cuban shores so the decision was made to unload her cargo on a deserted island in the Florida Keys. Her human cargo, consisting of the captain and crew, journalist Ralph Paine, various Cuban patriots, and a sharpshooter named Mike Walsh who had been offered $1000 in cash for each Spanish officer he killed, debarked in Key West where, on Christmas Day, 1896, they were greeted and wined and dined as heroes.

The rich contraband stashed by the *Three Friends* on No Name Island was later retrieved by the *Dauntless* and delivered to patriots in Cuba. The No Name Island recovery was only one of many adventures of the noted Captain Jim Floyd, African American skipper of the *Dauntless,* and his white crew, one of the most successful of the filibustering outfits. The magnificent sword that Hearst had commissioned and sent to Cuba on the *Three Friends* finally made it to General Maximo Gomez, but not until the war was over.

Newspapers printed exaggerated stories of the filibustering activities and made heroes of the captains running the blockade. Napoleon Broward, one of the "three friends," became such a hero throughout the pro-Cuban state of Florida that he was elected governor in 1905. Stephen Crane, the famous writer, came to Jacksonville, and probably also to Fernandina, to glean stories for his newspaper, even to the extent of signing on as seaman on the *Commodore*. The *Commodore* was an aging steamer that had been loaded in Jacksonville in full daylight with boxes of rifles and ammunition. Cuban supporters watching from the dock applauded and sang "strange patriotic songs" as the loading went on. In what was undoubtedly Crane's most exciting newspaper story, he described his first-hand experience of abandoning the *Commodore* when she sprung a leak and spending two nights and a day in a dingy with the captain and two crewmen before being rescued from the stormy seas. His adventures were later the basis for his noted short story "The Open Boat."

Several generations of Fernandinians have listened to and retold the true as well as the titillating stories of citizens caught up in filibustering intrigue. Almost forty years later,

Filibusters on the ship Three Friends in 1896.

Florida Memory Project
Florida Department of State
NO 40916

Alice Youngblood's *Seeing Fernandina* research notes record, "It is not well to mention names of people, so I am told. Persons telling me these stories asked me not to have any names mentioned, such as the Bordens, Baltzells." But the stories survive, none told with more glee than those told about Colonel Nathaniel Barnett Borden, the lumber factor who was instrumental in developing the "Fernandina Plan."

During the early filibustering years when he was Cuban Vice Consul, Borden kept an office in Havana. A romantic story is told of Borden's marriage to the beautiful and very young Florence Reynard. Flossie, as she was known, was the daughter of Captain Reynard, the owner and captain of a four-masted vessel with a sailing route from New York to Florida and the islands. While the Reynard ship was in port in Havana, Borden spirited the beautiful young Flossie away. According to notes found in Nancy Seibert's scrapbook now located in the Amelia Island Museum of History, Flossie and the Colonel then were married in the Catholic Cathedral in Havana and lived happily ever after in Fernandina. Colonel Borden built Villa las Palmas, one of Fernandina's grandest homes, for his wife in 1910.

Another wonderful story is still told in Fernandina relating to Borden's filibustering activities. In thanks for his ardent support of the Cuban cause, Borden was invited to Havana where he was entertained as a most honored guest and endowed with the title "Colonel." In the midst of the festivities, a Spanish don irate over Spain's loss of Cuba, challenged Borden to a duel. "Choose your weapons," he ordered. "Swords at sunrise," coolly responded the Colonel. But at sunrise, it is said, the Colonel was aboard a friendly Cuban fishing boat headed toward the safety of Key West. (Less romantically, some locals claim that the challenger was in fact a businessman angry over Borden's business practices.) Colonel Borden died on July 29, 1938, and was buried in Bosque Bello Cemetery.

In spite of the failure of Marti's efforts in Fernandina and his death in Cuba on May 9, 1895, the dashing exploits of the filibusterers appeared to ignite even greater American support for the Cuban rebels. Three years later, the explosion of the battleship *Maine* in the harbor of Havana infuriated pro-Cuban Americans, and on April 25, 1898, the United States declared war against Spain. The Treaty of Paris, signed December 10, 1898, made Marti's dream a reality.

Borden's beautiful mansion, Villa las Palmas still stands as a monument to filibustering in Fernandina and to his love for the charming Flossie. The *Three Friends*, sadly, lies on the bottom of the Saint Johns River. The heritage of Spanish Fernandina's smugglers, her Confederate blockade runners, and gallant filibusterers, however, did not die, but lived on in Prohibition-era rum runners and latter day shrimp boats that, rumor has it, sometimes returned to port laden with lucrative bales of marijuana along with their cargoes of shrimp.

Wars and Alarums
The Spanish American War - 1898

The action-packed filibustering years came to an end on Amelia Island when, on February 15, 1898, the U. S. S. *Maine* was blown to bits in Havana Harbor. On April 25, 1898, the United States officially declared war against Spain and the filibusters' support of Cuban rebels was illegal no more. There was much excitement in the port of Fernandina over the outbreak of the war, "a splendid little war" as Secretary of State John Hay famously called it. Floridians immediately demanded protection for their coast. Three days after the declaration of war, the War Department sent Captain John F. Honeycutt and Battery A of the 6th Artillery to Fort Clinch.

Fort Clinch had been vacant and under caretaker status since 1869, when the last Federal troops withdrew following the Civil War. Despite the fort's shoddy and still unfinished condition when Captain Honeycutt arrived in April, the capable officer soon managed to recondition antiquated guns, acquire new ones, raise a flag pole, remove tons of sand from the fort's barracks, officers' quarters, and parade ground, and dig an artesian well. According to letters from Captain Honeycutt to the Chief Quartermaster and Adjutant General of the Department of the Gulf, United States Army, Captain Honeycutt found the stagnant water standing in the fort "a menace to health." The sewer pipes from the Civil War occupation had all filled with sand. After much deliberation, "it was decided to cut an opening in the fort wall to a privy to be built just outside the fort." Since there was also no source of potable drinking water, Honeycutt ordered his men to dig a well.

To add to his drinking water and plumbing woes, Captain Honeycutt found Fort Clinch's Civil War-era guns and their carriages antiquated and practically useless. He struggled to put the fort in order with 209 poorly trained volunteers, all from Albany, New York. Some of the volunteers had entered the service to escape a severe economic recession, enlisting just to find food and housing. Honeycutt complained in a letter to the Adjutant General that many of his recruits were of a "low order of mentality, and 10% of them should be discharged." Among those in the 10%, one recruit was "almost idiotic;" one recruit was "dirty in person and habits;" one of the men was "too old," one was "deaf," and "all of the above recruits" were characterized by Honeycutt as "by far worse than the worst specimens I have ever seen in the army."

The declaration of war against Spain finally made it legal to ship troops and supplies to Cuba, and Fernandinians, having lately given up filibustering, demanded a bigger share of the military pie. A committee composed of E. D. Lukenbill, Judge H. J. Baker, and Mayor John McGiffin pressured Washington to choose Amelia Island as an embarkation site for U. S. soldiers and supplies being sent to Cuba and to establish an additional military encampment to supplement the small one that Honeycutt had already established at Fort Clinch. The committee's efforts appeared unproductive until its members produced a pamphlet outlining the advantages of Fernandina. The pamphlet extolled the healthful climate of Fernandina, its deepwater port, its nearness to the beach where bathing and drilling could take place, and its pure and abundant water supply. Evidently, the pamphlet was convincing to the War Department and a second encampment, called Camp Amelia,

AIMH

The Spanish American War brought back memories of the American Civil War as federal troops crowded Centre Street from the docks to Camp Amelia at the center of the island. Troops arrived by rail, were given minimal training, then many shipped out by steamer from the city's pier facilities to Cuba. Most, however, never made it off of the island as the conflict came to an early conclusion.

AIMH

was soon established on "the Lighthouse Reserve" near McClure's Hill. Although the war was over by August, over ten thousand volunteers, equivalent to the entire population of Nassau County, were eventually moved to the island.

When an unusually heavy rainfall in Tampa made a mud swamp of the military encampment there, many troops were transferred to Fernandina. They arrived at Camp Amelia on July 25, 1898, to do battle, not with mud as in Tampa, but with swarms of mosquitoes and a broiling July sun. The "pure and plentiful" water supply promised by the committee of prominent Fernandina citizens evoked loud

Camp Amelia as seen from the Amelia lighthouse.

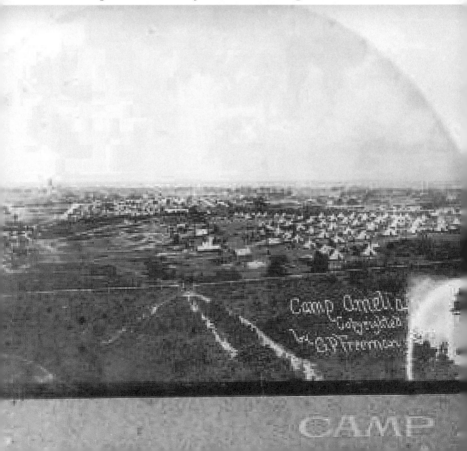

and long complaints about the sulfuric water's rotten-egg smell and taste. The pamphlet had promised temperatures "accompanied by a delicious cool breeze from the sea," but the troops, still wearing wool uniforms with wound cloth leggings (a contract for cotton uniforms had not yet been filled), complained bitterly of the intense heat on the treeless hill of the Lighthouse Reserve.

The photograph below of the era shows hundreds of small tents from the Lighthouse Reserve west to McClure's Hill. Careless attention to sanitation at the new camp soon resulted in alarming cases of typhoid fever among the troops. Some of the soldiers of Camp Amelia now

AIMH

rest, far from home, in their special plot in Bosque Bello cemetery—victims, not of the guns of war, but typhoid fever. An outbreak of measles further added to the miserable state of health of the men. The illnesses of the men were so widespread that even the most ordinary camp activities had to be curtailed. In an effort to combat heat exhaustion, all active work was suspended between 10 a.m. and 4 p.m. Fortunately for the troops, the war with Spain was brief. The armistice was signed on August 12, 1898, and, according to military records, on August 22, the troops left Fernandina for Huntsville, Alabama. Saint Michael's Church records record that Father Foley in 1898 "cared for the Catholic soldiers of the 69th New York and 8th Michigan regiments and offered an impressive military mass before the troops departed for other points." *Seeing Fernandina* reported that other soldiers stayed for sixteen weeks longer in the Fort Clinch installation.

On October 2, 1898, when only a few soldiers remained on the island, Amelia Island experienced a fierce hurricane. Of those who remained, most were convalescing from the earlier typhoid epidemic at a hospital established at the beach. Some of the soldiers were heroes of the storm as they assisted stranded beach dwellers in their efforts to cross flooded Egans Creek. Father Benedict, in his "Brief History of Churches of the Diocese of St Augustine," mentioned that soldiers from the Spanish American War, undoubtedly including these invalids, were cared for during the aftermath of the hurricane in St Michael's Hall.

The brief story of Fernandina and the Spanish American War ends with the Treaty of Paris, signed on December 10, 1898, in which Spain gave up all claims to Cuba. José Marti's dream of an independent Cuba soon became a reality.

Wars and Alarums
The Hurricane of 1898

Shortly after the armistice that ended the Spanish American War, Fernandina's waning economic prosperity suffered another blow on October 2, 1898, when a hurricane bringing an estimated fourteen-foot storm surge, the highest of local record, and northwest winds of ninety to one hundred miles per hour made landfall just to the north of Amelia Island between St. Marys and Woodbine in Camden County, Georgia. A full moon bringing high tides appeared on September 29th, and tides had also been higher than normal due to a Northeaster that had blown for several days. The onslaught of the storm, however, was sudden. The *Florida Mirror* reported in its first issue after the storm that at seven p.m. the wind was clocked at forty miles per hour from the northwest, but "Between eight and nine o'clock the wind had reached a velocity of 90 or 100 miles per hour." A barometer recorded pressure of 29.02, or 982.7mb. (Normal pressure at sea level is 1000 mb.) Eight feet of water was reported at Fort Clinch and the railroad depot was completely destroyed. The storm, now presumed to be a Category 4 hurricane, cost an estimated 179 lives as its full force hit northeast Florida and the Georgia coast.

The *Mirror* vividly noted the destruction Fernandina experienced:

> Centre street dock appeared to be in the midst of the pandemonium. This dock had a half dozen houses

The 1898 hurricane left no part of the island undamaged. Centre Street, above, saw major structural failure and near obliteration of the dock and rail facilities. Below, destruction of warehouses brought the town's economy to a halt.

upon it, the Mallory steamship office and four other houses occupied as restaurants and fish markets, and Kelly's warehouse, which was packed with hay, grain, flour and large quantities of canned goods. The F.C. & P. ticket office, baggage room and store room also occupied space on this dock. When the hurricane and tidal wave struck this structure there was not a piece of lumber left standing to mark the place where the dock stood. Cords of wood, bales of hay, barrels of flour and cased goods of descriptions were washed up Centre and other streets, several barrels of flour floated as far as the jail yard. The tug Gladiator was picked and placed securely on the bank between the pilings which once served as a support of the dock. The water invaded every building as high as Third street....As far as the eye can reach there can be nothing seen but one solid mass of lumber, logs and wreckage along where the tracks of the F.C. & P were once located.

Only one dock survived; the Quarantine Station was totally destroyed; live oaks were "twisted into small fragments;" and boats were thrown up into the St. Marys marshes. On Cumberland Island, the pilot boat *Maud Helen* was cast up on a twenty foot bluff, a dramatic sign of the hurricane's powerful storm surge. The Egmont Hotel's roof was "in the street." The *Mirror* also reported on heavy losses among Fernandina's black population: "The A.M.E. church on Beech street was torn up into splinters. These people had last Friday paid $500 as their last installment and were congratulating themselves as being free from debt; the building cost $3,500. The Good Templars' Hall and the Young Benevolent Hall belonging to colored societies were both annihilated." Amelia Beach suffered significant damage and most of its buildings were swept away. "The Strathmore

Hotel, the pavilions, the picturesque cottages at Amelia Beach now exist only in Memory—all were sacrificed to the storm's fury," the *Mirror* reported. (In fact, one of the new beach cottages and a portion of the Strathmore, later converted to a casino, did survive.)

Although the new National Weather Bureau's hurricane warning network established by President McKinley that summer had duly sounded an alert, warnings failed to reach some Fernandina residents summering at Amelia Beach, as well as sixty soldiers and two nurses, Misses Dunn and Wood, who were stationed at a hospital unit on the beach in the aftermath of the Spanish American War. The Army hospital unit's mules and horses tethered on the north side of the shell road were cut loose and narrowly escaped drowning in the storm's flood. A railroad engine and car were sent from Fernandina to rescue those stranded on the beach, including Judge H. J. Baker and his family, H. E. Dotterer and his family, and Mrs. G. T. Baltzell and her children. "The soldiers assisted the ladies and children into the car" but it was impossible to get the train back across flooded Egans Creek. Beach residents sought shelter as best they could. Nannie Yulee Baker Hardee, daughter of Judge Baker, recalled to a granddaughter taking her horse into the sand dunes hoping it would survive the storm. Her family later spent the night with her family at the cabin of Jimmy Drummond in the woods near Fort Clinch. As the winds abated, the storm victims were eventually rescued by boat.

In all, the *Mirror* tallied damages of over $250,000 throughout Fernandina and Amelia Beach. Mercifully, only two lives, the wife and child of Peter Armstrong of "Pigeon Point," were lost on Amelia Island. The *Mirror* concluded its saga, "This storm is without parallel in the history of Fernandina. None of our citizens had any storm or wind clause in their policies, which fact makes their losses so heavy."

The Last Glimmers of the Golden Age
The Palace Saloon

The enduring Palace opened in 1903 and still maintains it reputation, described by writer Al Burt in *Becalmed in the Mullet Latitudes*, as "the raunchiest and ritziest place to go" on Amelia Island. Not all of Fernandina's Golden Age social life centered on decorous church outings and society balls. Among the many waterfront saloons that served Fernandina's railroad men, dock workers, and fishermen, not to mention businessmen with a yen for a pint, the Palace Saloon was premiere. Much of the following information on Palace Saloon history is found in the now-rare publication entitled *Palace Saloon*. This elegant booklet, compiled by the noted local historian and author, Helen Gordon Litrico, was commissioned and published in 1981 by Land and Williams, Inc., and Palace owners Aubrey and Pat Williams. It was dedicated to the memory of previous owners Louis G. Hirth, Dee C. Land, and H. Erwin Williams.

The Palace, located on the northwest corner of Centre and Second Streets, claims the distinction of being Florida's oldest saloon. Josiah H. Prescott built the original structure in 1878, and W. H. Scott held the mortgage. The first business located in Prescott's fine "brick block" building was the Fernandina Cash Boot and Shoe Store.

Louis G. Hirth, a young German immigrant, purchased Prescott's well-constructed building with its six-foot deep oyster shell foundation in 1901. Hirth envisioned an

Louis G. Hirth, a visionary and entrepreneur, founded the Palace Saloon, and catered to all from rowdy sailors and old sea captains, to the elite of Cumberland Island and the rich and famous from around the world.

Centre Street and the Palace Saloon as they appeared the day before prohibition took effect. As one of the last towns in Florida to abide by the new Federal law, Fernandina sold most of the last stockpiled bottles of whiskey to bus loads of customers from Jacksonville.

establishment that would cater the local refined businessmen, visiting yachtsmen, and winter tourists rather than to railroad laborers and the rowdy sailors who swarmed ashore from the ships in the harbor to quench their thirsts at the waterfront saloons.

In essence, Hirth's vision was fulfilled, when through its long years of existence authors, artists, actors, Rockefellers, Carnegies, Vanderbilts, Goulds, duPonts, Henry Ford, Sam Goldwin, and Walter Cronkite, among others rich and famous, have bellied up to the English oak bar with its black mahogany caryatids smiling approval. Sea captains made themselves at home in the Palace, often playing cards around the clock, whiling away the hours and days in port while their ships were being loaded. Their crews, however, tended to spend their pay at the many other, less elegant, Fernandina bars. One of the local stories told about the early days of the Palace, however, is that during the famous "bluefish run" of 1912 and 1913, Scandinavian and Portuguese fishermen from the New Bedford area, following their catch to Amelia Island waters, jammed the Palace "200 at a time, in oilskins and boots, to drink and dance until there were so many fish scales on the floor it was hard to walk."

The Palace was in its heyday when Prohibition loomed on the horizon. The fight against demon rum had continued for decades. The Prohibition Party was organized in 1869; the Woman's Christian Temperance Union, in 1874; and the Anti-Saloon League, in 1893—all strong organizations with plenty of clout. Politicians, churches, country clubs, hotels, husbands, and wives chose up sides, and the nation-wide controversy went on and on until the federal government finally spoke. To the dismay of Palace owner Louis Hirth, the Temperance Movement was on the verge of victory.

But Louis Hirth was his name and booze was his game. If booze had to be outlawed by an act of Congress, then Hirth planned to go down in a blaze of glory. The masterful businessman Hirth had stockpiled carloads of whiskey and stored it in warehouses and boxcars against the fateful day when Prohibition was to become a reality. Reality came on January 16, 1919, with the ratification of the 18th Amendment to the Constitution of the United States. The Amendment gave the states, counties, and cities a year from the date of ratification to cease and desist in the manufacture, importation, exportation, and sale of intoxicating liquors.

Thanks to Hirth's foresight, Nassau County and Fernandina were the last county and town in the area to go bone-dry. As a consequence, trainloads, carloads, and bus loads of people came from Jacksonville and surrounding areas to make their final purchases of demon rum. Local stores sold out of suitcases, bags, baskets – anything that could hold the bottles. It is said that cars were backed up to Yulee on January 16, 1920' when Prohibition, if not Temperance, became the law of the land. An old photograph shows customers lined up, some with suitcases, to make their last legal purchases of whiskey from Hirth's North Second Street Huot-building warehouse. After these days of glory, the Palace was operated as an ice-cream parlor during the Prohibition years, but it struggled back to life again as a saloon when Prohibition was repealed.

Today's Palace is little changed from the original. The swinging doors announce the thirsty customer entering from the street. The same ornate light fixture gilt labeled "Palace," now moved indoors for safety, hangs over the bar. The cup hooks, once threaded from wall to wall with string festooned with coils of flypaper, are still there. There is the same tiled floor, the same pressed tin ceiling, once white but brown now with years of tobacco fumes, and the same long, handsome bar. The same murals on the walls still educate and delight customers with swashbuckling pirates and a soupçon of Latin, Shakespeare, and Dickens. Sometimes even inveterate teetotalers push open the swinging doors just to see the murals. Painted in 1907 by local painter Roy Kennard, the

The Palace Saloon circa 1961.

murals were restored in 1958 by the same artist.

However, there are a few changes. The fourteen-pound cuspidors, thankfully, are no longer in demand. The row of towels once hitched to the bar for mopping moustaches and overflowing beer are gone. The pot-bellied heating system has turned into a heat pump, and the round windows are permanently closed to keep in the air-conditioned coolness. The marble tables with the swing-out seats are now located in the porch rooms and kitchens of local citizens. One thing, however, that never changes about the Palace is the feeling a customer has of being in the presence of the past. Helen Litrico, in *Palace Saloon*, used a quote by Charles Brock from the *Florida Times Journal Magazine* of July 25, 1971, which seems to sum up this feeling:

> *The Palace Saloon is suffused with the past. You see it almost through a sepia tint. When you stride through the swinging doors, you somehow feel you are sporting a handlebar moustache. You belly up to the solid oak, hand-carved bar, and the bartender slides a mug of suds to you, and ghosts from ten decades join in drinking to your health....*

The Last Glimmers of the Golden Age
The Post Office

Without question, the United States post office on the corner of Centre and Fourth Streets is the finest of Amelia Island's civic buildings and the architectural crown of Fernandina's dying Golden Age.

According to a history of the Fernandina post office by former Postmaster Louis Goldstein, early records indicate that two soldiers in 1817 regularly brought mail to Fernandina from Saint Augustine. From Fernandina, Farquar Bethune delivered the mail to Saint Marys. The first real post office on Amelia Island, however, was established September 22, 1821, with Domingo Acosta as its first postmaster. According to records of the Research Administrator/Historian of the office of the Postmaster General, postal service was discontinued on May 23, 1844, and reinstated on May 11, 1855, with Amaziah Coy as postmaster. For a brief period during the Civil War, the postal system once again ceased operations from October 25, 1862, until its reestablishment on April 27, 1863. In 1896, the postal service operated from the downtown business establishment of Frank Simmons at 212 Centre Street.

In 1907, while Oliver S. Oakes served as postmaster, the U. S. government purchased land for a new building to house both a post office and Federal court offices. James Knox Taylor, supervising architect for the United States Treasury department, was its designer and the D. J. Phipps Co. of

AIMH

A peaceful Centre Street looking past the recently completed Federal Building (above) looking to the west toward the docks five blocks away. The building (as shown below) has served as a courthouse, customs house, military recruiting office and post office.

AIMH

Newport News, Virginia, handled the building's construction. Groundbreaking for the new structure took place on April 2, 1909, and by October 1910, photographs now in the collections of the Amelia Island Museum of History show a finished lobby. Evidently the post office was in use for over a year before its official dedication in 1912.

According to Fernandina's Historic American Building Survey conducted in 1974, architect James Taylor chose a Mediterranean type of architecture popular in Florida in the early twentieth century. A graceful marble staircase led to the high-ceilinged second floor courtroom. The roof, corbels, decorative iron, oak trim, and plaster work are outstanding architectural elements. Until recent years, cast-metal lamp standards adorned the entrances of the building, but when one was accidentally damaged, all four were removed. Efforts by Amelia Island preservationists have been successful in having two of the standards replaced at the Centre Street entrance.

The Post Office building served as a Customs House as well as housing military recruiting offices and court rooms. Federal processes such as Admiralty and Customs courts were heard in the exquisite federal courtroom on the second floor. Fernandina old timers recall that during Prohibition, bottles of illegal whiskey used as evidence in bootlegging trials were emptied after the verdicts, and, according to I. W. Hardee, Jr., in a conversation with his daughter, Fernandina residents "brought sponges" to collect the spilled whiskey.

Update

In recent years the post office building's court room was thoughtlessly stripped of its furnishings to the dismay of local citizens. According to the *Fernandina News-Leader* of

October 19, 1984, Judge William Terrell Hodges, chief judge of the Middle District of Florida, visited the Fernandina Post Office and found "a wealth of antique furniture, chairs, desks, armoires, and a witness box." According to the *News-Leader* article, Judge Hodges is quoted as saying in a telephone interview, "The furniture was in a state of disrepair so I arranged to have it removed. I have an interest in preserving what is old and what is good and much of the furniture in Fernandina qualified." Included in the same newspaper article is a photograph showing sturdy oak furniture in apparently perfect condition being loaded into a moving van. Fortunately, a small portion of the furnishings have been returned.

Historic American Building Survey

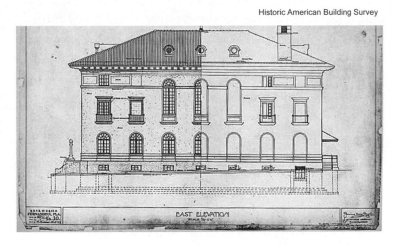

The east facade as drawn for the Historic American Building Survey.

The Last Glimmers of the Golden Age
The Keystone Hotel

Nothing could have jarred the citizens of Amelia Island into a true appreciation of the architectural heritage of the town of Fernandina and a strong will to preserve it than the demolition in 1974 of the Keystone Hotel. Even after years have passed, to some it is still a shock to return to Fernandina from out of town and find the Ludowici roof-tiled Keystone Hotel vanished from the landscape. The hotel, described in the *Fernandina News Record* on July 9, 1915, featured a wide awning-shaded verandah extending across the Centre Street length of the building; electric fans cooling the public rooms; and a garage to accommodate twenty-five cars. Bright red colored tile shaped like keystones decorated the facade.

Prominent Fernandina citizens formed a stock company to build the hotel. Most active in the venture were L. G. Hirth, Effingham W. Bailey, J. H. McGiffin, and John Mann. John Mann was the builder and John McGiffin donated the land. When subscriptions were not forthcoming as pledged, Hirth and Bailey ended up as sole owners of the fine new three-story, thirty-two room hotel. On May 28, 1915, the *Fernandina News Record* reported that Hirth and Bailey hired Mr. Roy A. Talbot, described as being "the youngest hotel manager in the state," to manage the facility. According to the *News-Record* of June 4, 1915, the Keystone planned to open

The Keystone Hotel was the flagship of Amelia Island hotels for 50 years, replacing the glamor of the short lived Egmont Hotel. From high-cotton island society to Sunday brunchers, to high school proms, the Keystone was Amelia's premier hotel until her unfortunate demise in 1974.

its doors on June 10 with celebrations including a grand ball, dinner from 6:30 to 8, and dancing beginning at 9 o'clock. Large automobile parties from Jacksonville were expected, and "Mr. George A. Gray, a celebrated airman" served as the featured attraction. Mr. Gray planned to fly up from Saint Augustine and "give exhibits of aerial navigation."

The *Fernandina News-Record,* on July 20, 1915, announced that the hotel had purchased a "beautiful new Victrola." The hotel was noted for its food, and delicious meals were sent up by dumb waiters from the basement kitchen to the main-floor dining room. An extensive guest list appeared in the weekly newspaper. Dances were held every Tuesday and Saturday evenings.

Unfortunately for the Keystone's future success, only one of the thirty-two rooms had a private bath, a typical arrangement for a hotel of the time. Most of the rooms shared a bath with the room next door. There was no elevator, just the dumb waiter to serve the dining room. Pens and kitchen gardens located behind the hotel supplied the dining room with poultry and vegetables. Local citizens claim that during Prohibition a very private club in the basement level of the hotel was patronized by fearless locals and out-of-towners in search of adult beverages. (L. G. Hirth of Palace Saloon fame, a curious reader will note, was co-owner and sometime manager of the Keystone.) *Florida Earth*, a real estate magazine, in its August 21, 1925, "Fernandina Issue," ran an advertisement for the Keystone with the coy slogan, "the Hotel with a Reputation."

Among the hotel managers were owner L. G. Hirth; Albert Simon, whose wife ran the dining room; Mr. and Mrs. L. A. Klarcr, who purchased the hotel when Hirth died; a Mr. Johnson; a Mr. Spitler; Mr. and Mrs. George T. Davis; and Mr. and Mrs. George Fox.

The last spurt of activity in the life of the Keystone took place between 1957 and 1971, when baseball players from as many as six minor league teams stayed at the hotel during their spring training. The Charlotte Hornets was the main farm team of the Washington Senators, later becoming the Minnesota Twins. The Hornets and farm club players of the Baltimore Orioles were among the popular spring residents at the venerable Keystone. They could frequently be found enjoying the verandah's cool breezes in the afternoon after practices.

When it appeared that the Keystone had reached the end of her career as a hotel, there was much discussion about alternative uses for the building such as retirement apartments or city and county facilities. Regrettably, the wrecking ball won out, and the death knell of the Keystone tolled. As a result of the shocking demolition of the Keystone Hotel, a small preservation-minded group of citizens organized the Fernandina Amelia Island Restoration Foundation. This organization continues to be a strong advocate for the preservation of the outstanding architectural heritage of Fernandina and Amelia Island.

The Last Glimmers of the Golden Age
Into the New Century

The Keystone Hotel's opening procession of automobiles and "exhibits of aerial navigation" confirmed Fernandina's arrival in the twentieth century. Like the Keystone, however, the town failed to thrive with the passing years. While most of Florida reaped the fruits of the boom years of the early 1920s, Fernandina's economy was stagnant, its population barely changing. A few historic Fernandina buildings were lost to fire, a few converted into apartments, and many sunk into genteel shabbiness.

In the midst of the Great Depression, however, several developments occurred that had implications for a more prosperous future. In 1936, the Florida government purchased Fort Clinch and much of its surrounding property, land that had been sold by the Federal government to private owners in 1926. For two years, Civilian Conservation Corps crews undertook restoration and improvements on the old fort and surrounding area that are still enjoyed today. Fort Clinch opened as a state park in 1939. In 1937, Container Corporation of America opened a large pulp mill between "New Fernandina" and Old Town, and in 1938, Rayonier Corporation followed suit with a mill on the waterfront south of downtown. The pulp and paper industry thus established continues to employ hundreds of Fernandina residents. In

1935, A.L. Lewis, Afro-American Insurance executive from Jacksonville, founded American Beach. During the long years of segregation, American Beach thrived as one of Florida's few beaches for black residents and tourists.

During the World War II years, Fort Clinch was once again commissioned as a military installation, this time as a Coast Guard facility. Fernandina residents, including Suzanne Hardee, patrolled local beaches looking for German planes, ships, or submarines. Fernandina's coastal location made a stringent black-out imperative, and the Amelia Light, electrified in 1933, went dark for the duration. Peacetime brought the baby boom that required a new elementary and, a few years later, a new high school. By mid-century, population exceeded six thousand. The opening of the Buccaneer Trail in 1950 linked Amelia Island to points south and attracted tourists with its hints of the island's glamorous past. In 1952, local boosters succeeded in changing "Fernandina" to "Fernandina Beach."

The 1960s heralded the beginning of desegregation for Nassau County schools, Fernandina's first Shrimp Festival in 1963, and in 1964, another severe hurricane, Hurricane Dora. In 1971, planning began for the Amelia Island Plantation. Fernandina residents, in response to the destruction of the Keystone Hotel and the prospect of competition from the looming development of the south end of Amelia Island, worked for recognition of a 30-block area of Golden Age Fernandina as a Historic District in the National Register of Historic Places. Since the 1970s, the formerly working class town of pulp mills and shrimp boats has tried to come to terms with glossy developments, pricey historic renovations, and up-scale tourism.

Historic downtown Fernandina remains the jewel in Amelia's crown. Like Charleston or Savannah, Fernandina was fortunate to be poor during periods of bad architecture. The gracious Victorian charm of its downtown businesses and residences and the beauty of its rivers and beaches provide an unmatched quality of life that has propelled Fernandina's population to over 10,000 residents by the turn of the century. The lessons of the Golden Age, however, are not merely aesthetic. The selfless sacrifices of Chloe Merrick and her Freedman's Bureau teaching colleagues, the nuns of St. Joseph's convent who left far-away France to teach and nurse the poor of Fernandina, and the brave doctors who served yellow fever patients at their own peril still inspire us. The concern for the public good that led city leaders to establish schools, libraries, parks, and beach recreational opportunities challenges us today. The determination that led David Yulee and those who followed him to confront war, epidemics, storms, and economic set-backs with renewed energy and creativity is extraordinary. These, too, are part of Fernandina's Golden Age and its enduring legacy.

Index

Suzanne Hardee